Shine

A Girl's Guide to Thriving
(Not Just Surviving) in Real Life

Mary Doherty has taught English for fifteen years in the Ursuline Secondary School, Thurles, County Tipperary. Originally from Bray, County Wicklow, she studied English and History at UCD, graduating with a master's in Anglo-Irish Literature in 1992. She has also taught in Loreto, Bray, Castleknock College and Kilkenny College. She has been a class tutor for fifteen years, a role which she absolutely loves, and as a result has experienced many teenage issues first hand and gotten to know the girls on a very personal level. Mary is also a transition year coordinator and Learning Support teacher. She lives in Kilkenny with her husband and two children.

Siobhán Hackett, a graduate of Crawford College of Art in Cork with a Diploma in Educational Psychology, has many years' experience in dealing with teenagers. Her understanding of adolescents and the issues that trouble them has made her a source of comfort, wisdom and trust for young people. Added to this is her passionate interest in the many and differing ways that students learn which can often prevent them enjoying the experience of school life if left unaddressed. Siobhán is the Learning Support Coordinator at the Ursuline Secondary School, teaching Learning Support, Resource and Art. She lives in Tipperary with her husband and two children.

Shine

A Girl's Guide to Thriving
(Not Just Surviving) in Real Life

MARY DOHERTY AND SIOBHÁN HACKETT

HACHETTE
BOOKS
IRELAND

Abbreviations

Author's name: Mary (M) and Siobhán (S)

To Ray, Liam and Amy.

To Damian, Ava and Grace.

First published in 2015 by Hachette Books Ireland

A CIP catalogue record for this title is available from the British Library

ISBN: 978-1-4736-2268-5

Book design and typesetting: Anú Design, Tara
Printed and bound by CPI Group (UK) Ltd, Croydon, CR0 4YY

Hachette Books Ireland policy is to use papers that are natural, renewable and
recyclable products and made from wood grown in sustainable forests. The logging and
manufacturing processes are expected to conform to the environmental regulations of the
country of origin.

Hachette Books Ireland
8 Castlecourt Centre
Castleknock
Dublin 15, Ireland

A division of Hachette UK Ltd.
Carmelite House
50 Victoria Embankment,
London EC4Y 0DZ

www.hachette.ie

Contents

We would like to thank all the students who helped us with the chapter titles!

x

Introduction

> *'If there is one lesson that I have learned during my life on the planet it is this: the number one thing all people crave is to be seen and heard. It's just that simple.'*
>
> — Oprah Winfrey —

The inspiration for this book comes from all the wonderful and inspiring teenagers we have met over our thirty years of collective teaching. You have taught us so much about life and made us laugh out loud every day!

We are addressing the future movers and shakers of our country – the dreamers, the poets, the athletes, the musicians, the healers, the brain surgeons, the mothers, the CEOs and the friends. This book is for you.

Adolescence has often been described as an emotional assault course and for good reason. Over the years, students have come to us for support, advice and sometimes just a sympathetic ear. Our aim is to provide you with the necessary tools to overcome the most common teenage hurdles. Hopefully, after reading *Shine*, you will realise that you are not alone and that the problems or challenges that you may be facing right now are actually universal ones. All teenagers want to be validated. They want to be respected and treated fairly. As Oprah says, it really is that simple.

From the beginning, the scope of this book was enormous and very ambitious. We wanted to focus on the most common teenage issues but we also needed to keep things informative and concise. We firmly believe that if you know what is ahead of you, then you can manage things better.

Adolescents get a lot of bad press. You may wonder why your parents place so many demands and expectations on your shoulders and it's quite possible that you often feel that they don't understand you at all. This can be an anxious and uncertain time. However, it's important that you remember that even though your parents may not like your behaviour, they still love you and always will.

In life, there will be times when you go through challenging periods and come out the other side a little wiser if a bit bruised and battered. In this respect, we are all alike. If you stop to think about it for a moment a lot of the messages that you are being bombarded with on a daily basis are

misleading at best and damaging at worst. The media often presents us with a very artificial version of the world. If we are to believe everything we see or read, we might mistakenly think that everyone else's life is perfect (except ours), that we can only be truly happy if we are impossibly thin and beautiful and that there is something seriously wrong with us if we are single. Remember, girls – you can decide whether to buy into this illusion or not. You know how you want to live your life, you have the power to make decisions which are the right ones for you and you alone and ultimately you have the responsibility for your own happiness. Maybe it's time for you to acknowledge just how powerful you really are – understand that everyone has flaws and imperfections and embrace them. We believe that there is great power in acceptance.

We all want our dreams to come true. The definition of success is different for everyone. For some it is achieving their goals, for others it is the attainment of wealth and power. You are on your own journey so do not compare yourself to others. Never let anyone dull your sparkle. Believe in your strengths and abilities because everything you need to succeed lies within. Let your inner compass guide you. And, in the coming years as you discover who you are, remember you are the expert at being you. Step out of the shadows and let your amazing and true self SHINE!

Part One

Dear Me,
Today I Will Shine

Shiny Happy People

True friends make your life sparkle. They accept you for who you really are and embrace your individuality. You turn to them when you make mistakes because you know that they will understand you but never judge you. With them, you can laugh until your head hurts and your stomach aches – they make the world a brighter place and help you to feel much more secure. Real friends are like beacons shining in the darkness, offering hope and strength when your heart gets broken, when school becomes too much or when your parents are driving you crazy. The teenage years would stretch out like a vast wasteland if you had no wonderful people to join you on your journey. As the old saying goes, 'you can choose your friends but you can't choose your family' – so choose your friends very wisely indeed – and if you are very lucky, they may still be a part of your life in years to come…

'I have learned that
to be with those I like is enough.'
ﾟ◌ Walt Whitman ◌ﾟ

The value of friendship

We have all heard the famous expression 'No man is an island', from the poem of the same name by John Donne. If we are to truly give meaning to our lives, it is essential that we bond with other people because, after all, we are social creatures who all crave and need connectivity. The value of friendship is something we don't often take the time to fully appreciate. Your friends can keep your feet placed firmly on the ground and help you to keep life in perspective. They know exactly how quirky you are yet still want to go out with you on a Saturday night. It's important to point out at this early stage that we are talking about good old-fashioned real friends here and not virtual ones! It doesn't really matter if you have a thousand friends on Facebook, what is important is the quality of your friendships and whether they will be there during the good times and bad.

You begin the process of identity formation during your teenage years when your associations with like-minded people become very important to you. It is quite normal for you to want to spend more time with your friends and less time with your parents because you feel deep down that your friends are the ones who really understand you properly. (But don't ever forget, girls, that you have strong allies at home.) Having one or two loyal and trustworthy friends is essential because they are like a personal support group and can make you feel valued and validated. As well as that, they can teach you important life skills such as being sensitive to others' thoughts and feelings.

'Close friends are truly life's treasures.'

Vincent Van Gogh

Respect

This is a crucial ingredient in any relationship, whether it is platonic or romantic, because respect enables you to accept and love your friend for who they really are. True friends communicate openly, listen to each other's ideas and value each other's opinions even if they don't always agree with each other. By respecting a friend's time, freedom and individuality you pave the way for a solid and lasting relationship.

How to be a good friend

✳ Never disrespect your friends!

✳ Don't go green with envy when your best friend in the world makes new friends or if she finds a new love interest. You may feel a little left out but you have got to remember that she must be free to live her own life too. Never be afraid to give your friend a little space if you think that this is what she needs. When you take a step back, it's easier to understand that, although you may not see as much of her as you would like, she still cares for you just as much as ever. Don't crowd her.

What is a friend?
A single soul dwelling in two bodies.
Aristotle

★ If they tell you a secret from the depths of their soul don't talk about it with anyone else. If you do, you could lose their trust and, once it's gone, trust can be a tricky thing to get back. Gossiping devalues your friendship. Stop and ask yourself, 'Is this something I would want shared if the situation was reversed?'

★ Nobody wants to hang around with a drama queen so try not to be too demanding. If you are, your friend might think that you believe their time is less precious than yours. Appreciate that their time is valuable too.

★ Don't dismiss your friend's issues. Something that is trivial to you may be monumentally important to her. Try to understand what they may be feeling and be there for them.

★ Never ever involve others in your disagreements. If you have an argument with a friend, there is no need to tell everyone in your social circle about all the gory details in an attempt to 'rally the troops' so that you feel that you have everybody on your side. Keep things simple: go to the person you have the issue with and talk it out with them. Just because you are going through a difficult stage right now does not mean that you will never work through it.

★ Be trustworthy. Establishing a habit of lies to cover your tracks can result in negative consequences. So always be yourself – your friends will love you just as you are, no matter how weird or wonderful!

It is one of the blessings
of old friends that you can afford to
be stupid with them.
Ralph Waldo Emerson

✻ It's not a good idea to go out with your friend's ex without her permission. There is a tendency to like and desire the people who are familiar to us. If you are considering this, have a conversation with your friend about it first. You have to be willing not to pursue your crush if your friend is not comfortable about the idea and, let's face it, she probably won't be. At your age, the chances are that no boyfriend or girlfriend will be in your life as long as your friend will. **Never** fight over a man! During the teen years, loves come and go but a good friendship is priceless and can last forever.

'Friends ... they cherish one another's hopes.
They are kind to one another's dreams.'
✵ *Henry David Thoreau* ✵

Knowing a good friendship from a destructive one

In life, it is inevitable that you will come up against situations where you have to make difficult decisions about whether or not to give in to peer pressure. Good friends who have your best interests at heart can guide and help you when you are faced with challenging circumstances and situations. True friends respect you, look out for you, care for you and include you in activities. They are also not afraid to tell you the truth, even if you might not always like what they have to say.

A healthy friendship allows you to be yourself, brings you happiness and facilitates your growth as an individual. It makes you feel all warm and fuzzy inside. It also encourages and supports you so that you can become the best person possible. Remember, you don't have to talk or text each other every day – real friends are not afraid to give each other a generous amount of space and establish healthy boundaries. They listen when you need to say something and offer useful advice when they can.

However, not all friendships are positive. If you can at all, try to steer clear of negative or toxic friendships. Life is just too short for putting up with bitter, miserable people. If you get an overwhelming feeling that you can't be yourself when you are with a friend then alarm bells should ring. Trust your instincts – they are hardly ever wrong! If a 'friend' is making unreasonable demands and constantly leaves you feeling betrayed, hurt, disappointed or drained, then maybe it's time to stop and re-evaluate your friendship. Ask yourself a few simple questions like:

✳ How do my friends make me feel when I am with them?

✳ Do they include me in activities and make good decisions?

✳ Do my friends have my best interests at heart?

✳ Do I feel that I have to pretend to be someone I'm not when I'm with them or do I feel free to be myself?

✳ Do I like who I am when I spend time with my friends?

✳ Do I behave differently when I'm with the group? Do my values change? Why?

✳ Do I enjoy being with this group? If not, why not?

'I don't need a friend who changes when I change and who nods when I nod: my shadow does that much better.'

Plutarch

A healthy friendship encourages and supports you.

Making new friends

For some, making new friends can be difficult and challenging. The good news is that it doesn't have to be. Below are some simple tips from our students about how to make and keep good friends. Loneliness is painful, so putting time, energy and attention into trying these tips is worth your while if you wish to find and cultivate new friendships. Be brave, you can do this!

TIPS FOR MAKING AND KEEPING FRIENDS

✪ If you want to make friends you have to be yourself, pure and simple. No one likes a fraud. Do not try too hard to look or act cool.

✪ When you are chatting to people, be friendly and helpful. Be a good listener and value what they have to say about themselves and the world around them. It is a universal truth that people like to talk about themselves and their lives. So show interest and give them your undivided attention. They'll love you for it!

✪ Questions are the perfect icebreaker as they give the other person a chance to talk, then they in turn can ask you a question. Saying something simple like 'Where did you get your shoes? I love them!' could be all you need to do to start an interesting and rewarding connection.

✪ Based on your interests and strengths, check out activities, clubs and teams at school or in your local area. By joining the group you are providing an opportunity to connect with like-minded people.

✪ Laughter plays an essential role in building strong, fun friendships. Develop a good sense of humour and don't over-react to teasing.

✪ Whatever you do, try not to appear standoffish and cold. Smile brightly and look people in the eyes. By doing this you will appear approachable and warm and people will be more likely to come over for a chat. Confidence is very attractive!

✪ Take it slowly. Let friendships develop gradually. Do not overwhelm the other person by crowding them. A needy friend can be a big turnoff.

✪ It is hard to be around people who complain about everything. We all know that negativity can be seductive and it's easy to focus on what is difficult. Be positive and grateful – these are much nicer qualities.

✪ Be open-minded when making friends. Don't be judgemental. Look for the good in others. No one is perfect. Remind yourself that you too have faults.

> **Be yourself and the right people will accept you for who you are.**

We don't meet people by accident.
They are meant to cross our path for a reason.
:◌ Unknown ◌:

Making and keeping friends can be difficult if you are shy or unsure of yourself. You may be uncomfortable with the thought of approaching someone else. Rehearse ahead of time if that will make you feel more relaxed and less apprehensive. With the help of your parents, role play ways to approach other teens, introduce yourself and keep a conversation flowing.

Be available when you can, as friendships grow when we make time to do things together. Invite friends to go out with you or hang around at the weekend so that you can have fun together.

There is only so much you can do for a friend, so if they have serious problems or are taking grave risks, be careful. You cannot be expected to fix everything. You may need to seek outside help from a family member or a teacher. Supporting a friend through difficult periods can put pressure on you, so make sure to take care of yourself too.

When friendship goes bad

'I choose my friends carefully.'
:◌ Barack Obama ◌:

Every friendship has minor ups and downs but genuine friendships go the distance. Friendships change; sometimes they fade and naturally drift apart as you just don't connect like you once did. Others end abruptly and can leave you feeling like the wind has been taken out of your sails.

Sadly, the people who know you best are also the ones who have the most power to hurt you. So when trust is repeatedly broken or your friend is consistently inconsiderate of your feelings or enjoys humiliating you publicly, it really is time to take a step back and re-evaluate what the friendship really means to you.

Friendships can fail for many different reasons – jealousy or betrayal might creep in and destroy what you once had. A friend can quickly become a 'frenemy'. Friendship should never cause more stress than pleasure. You have the right to stand up for what you believe in. Say 'No' if you disagree with someone. Don't be afraid to stand on your own two feet – in the long run, people will respect you more when you do so. If you are genuinely afraid of losing a friendship because you are expressing your beliefs then maybe your friendship was unstable in the first place. It is unhealthy for your development if a friendship makes you feel worse about yourself, rather than better. A genuine friend will allow you to shine and encourage you to succeed.

There appears to be an unwritten law that makes us believe that we must remain friends with everyone, even when the friendship is unsupportive, degrading and toxic. Just as you would end a romantic relationship when the love has gone, it is also sometimes necessary to end friendships that have turned sour. Some people find it best to let the friendship just fade out gradually while others find that an open conversation is the best way to finish things. Be kind and forgiving whatever you do. Stay positive. New and wonderful friends will come into your life – you just have to be open to receiving them!

True friends love you for who you are.

At times, friendships may seem to take a lot of effort, but the hard work is worth it when you form amazing and life-enhancing bonds with fabulous people. Friends help us to live more fulfilling lives. What a person looks like or what clothes they wear are unimportant. It is what's on the inside that counts.

Friends support and empower you. But you have a responsibility to be there for them too, even when the going gets tough. Take care of yourself, value your friends and shine like the star that you are.

Peer pressure

'Be yourself, everyone else is already taken.'
Oscar Wilde

Negative peer pressure is doing something you know you shouldn't, such as skipping class, smoking, drinking and doing drugs. There can be serious risks involved. How young people decide to handle this pressure can influence their lives significantly. A teenager said to us recently, 'I don't always feel confident enough in my own skin to disagree with my peers.' Being accepted by a peer group can seem more important than doing what parents want or doing the right or safe thing.

If you are feeling pressured and finding it difficult to resist, we urge you to please stop, think and ask yourself these questions, because true friends would not ask you to do anything that could harm you in any way.

✴ What are the long-term effects of my actions on my self-esteem?

✴ Could I be physically harmed? Could someone else be hurt by my actions?

✴ Will my behaviour damage my relationship with my family?

✴ Is this against the law?

In order to become a responsible adult, you must stand up for what you believe in, even when friends and peers disagree with you. You know right from wrong and you must decide which path to venture down. If you are strong enough to do what you know is right, you can influence the whole group in a very positive way. Believe in yourself – do not do things that make you uncomfortable. Try to assess the risks ahead of time. Look ahead to the consequences. Make concrete decisions about life. Don't be afraid to say 'No'.

'This above all: to thine own self be true.'

William Shakespeare, 'Hamlet'

All You Need
is Love

Relationships change, especially romantic ones. When you are growing up your relationships are vitally important but at the same time not without challenges. You could find that you gravitate towards certain people because you simply have more in common with them and view the world in a similar vein, whereas sadly you may drift apart from others for all sorts of reasons. This happens – friends and boyfriends and girlfriends will come in and out of your life like actors walking on and off a stage. You do not need to be friends with the whole world in order to be happy. If you have a few close relationships with people who respect and love you exactly how you are, then count yourself very lucky and cherish them and hold them close to your heart. However, if you find yourself in an unhealthy or toxic relationship which leaves you feeling controlled, disrespected, uneasy or even unsafe, do yourself a big favour and walk away with your head held high.

What is a healthy relationship?

A healthy relationship should be built on:

1. **Trust** – of course it is natural to get a little jealous at times, but if your partner gets angry every time you are talking to another boy or girl, warning bells should begin to ring. It is impossible to have a healthy relationship if you do not trust each other. Do not mistake excessive jealousy with intense feelings of care or concern. Controlling behaviour or violence of any sort are never OK and you should not tolerate them.

2. **Respect** – you have to value your partner for who they really are. Understand that boundaries are necessary for both of you. Treat each other well. Try not to disrespect each other when in the company of friends.

3. **Honesty** – do not play games. The truth is always a straight course. Lies tie us up in knots and make life very complicated indeed.

4. **Equality** – be fair to each other and make sure there is a balance when it comes to making decisions like what movie to go to on a Saturday night or whose house to hang out in mid-week. Spend time with your partner's friends and yours. Do not ignore your own friends because of your new love; they will not thank you for this!

 21

5. **Support** – be there for each other through the rough and the smooth.

6. **Space** – in a healthy relationship it's important to spend time together and get to know each other, but you also need time apart. Remember absence can make the heart grow fonder!

7. **Open communication** – talk, even if you are afraid that what you have to say may not be what your partner wants to hear. Always speak honestly so that miscommunication is avoided.

Finding the right person

In order to find the perfect person for you, it is important to be clear in your mind about what you want and what you need in a partner. These are two different things entirely – **wants** include the things that you think you would like in a boyfriend or girlfriend: for example, you might think that he or she has to be tall, gorgeous, rich and with brains to burn. **Needs** are different and generally they don't tend to change – you will always need a partner who is kind and caring. Some things may appear to be crucially important to you at first, but as time goes on you may find that keeping an open mind when it comes to discovering who is partner material is the best way forward. It could be possible that the person for you is cute on the looks scale rather than drop-dead gorgeous. If he/she makes you laugh and worships the ground you walk on, chances are that they are a much better proposition than someone who looks like they've just stepped out of a magazine but is only interested in their hair and bores you half to death.

When they don't love you back

'I am hurting so badly since they left – what can I do? ... How do I start to move on?'

Falling in love is an exhilarating feeling, but when love ends, it can feel like you have been floored by an emotional tidal wave. It's all-consuming and it can feel like the end of the world.

When faced with a break-up, you may be overcome with feelings of hurt, disappointment, anger or embarrassment. Anxiety can creep in. Thankfully, we are all different. Some people prefer blondes rather than brunettes while others prefer chatty individuals over quiet ones. Embrace and accept yourself just as you are and don't try to change yourself for anyone. Instead, keep reminding yourself that the perfect relationship just hasn't come your way yet.

Whether your relationship was long term or only lasted a couple of months, pain is pain. Sometimes it can be hard to imagine that you will ever feel better; the misery you feel could be overwhelming and may even seem insurmountable. Be patient and gentle – give yourself some time out and allow healing to take its course. Don't rush back into a relationship just because you can't cope with being alone. The likelihood of a rebound relationship lasting is low anyway because you are only dragging emotional baggage and bruises along with you. Keep your mind centred on the present and avoid reliving the past or worrying about the future. The truth is, when you let go, you allow the healing process to speed up.

Not all relationships are meant to last forever, so when yours ends, don't feel too rejected. Acknowledge your feelings, but do not dwell on them obsessively. If you can, be philosophical and view the split as a learning experience. Often, a break-up can be the catalyst for personal growth, a time to observe and heal your issues, learn important life lessons and discover how to open your heart and love again. You cannot gain something in life without losing something first, so make way for new and wonderful people and experiences to come in to your life.

Change makes our journey through life more interesting and exciting. Embrace these challenges and accept that every relationship teaches you something about yourself and others.

**Do not be afraid to move on.
Open your heart and love again.**

'It takes courage to love.'

Eleanor Roosevelt

Everyone can remember their first relationship and the rush of emotions and excitement that accompanied it. First love is a heady mixture of agony and ecstasy – some of the greatest songs and books have been written about it and rightly so. Try to enjoy your teenage romances; view them as fun and enjoyable learning experiences. One student described her relationship break-up very eloquently when she said, 'I know it's clichéd but it is like my world has been ripped in two, the glue that held it together has been torn apart.'

(S) I remember a student crying in my classroom as she told me that because of her break-up she honestly felt that her life had ended. She could completely identify with the phrase 'love is a drug', the feelings of hopelessness, anxiety, sleeplessness and pain were very real and tangible. She felt so unmotivated and lethargic. She commented that her parents didn't know what to do to help her. She thought that she would never be happy or find love again. Now, many months on, she realises that although it did take a while for her sadness to go away, all heartbreak heals in time. Be patient and kind with yourself girls – the pain will go and you will love again.

(M) Another student described her hurt after a break-up. She didn't realise just how much love can hurt. It wasn't that she stopped loving him, it was just that she no longer felt the same way about him. She claimed that it would have been easier to finish the relationship if he had treated her badly, but he didn't. He was the perfect gentleman. She was fearful that people would think her heartless and cold. I advised her to follow her heart and try not to worry what others think, because sometimes relationships just run their course and we all have to accept that.

When you experience the hurt of a break-up, it's easy to say that you are finished with love. The fear of getting hurt again is very real. Stop! Falling in love has an element of **risk** built in, but of course **it is worth it.** As Alfred Tennyson once wrote, ''Tis better to have loved and lost than never to have loved at all.' These are wise words and the alternative – to never love again – is not even worth contemplating.

You may feel like your heart has been broken into a million pieces, but once you come through the hurt and pain – and you will – you will realise that you have the strength to get through anything.

You are strong and you will get through it.

'Never love anyone who treats you
like you are ordinary.'
~ Oscar Wilde ~

Navigating heartbreak on social media

Most of us know from personal experience that a relationship break-up can create temporary feelings of rejection, pain and self-doubt. When we are hurting, we sometimes say things that later we regret. If you can, try to stay away from social media after a split and take a break from technology. Yes, you **can** do it! You do **not** need to broadcast your relationship status online. Try to deal with your grief and anger by talking to someone you trust. We can all heal and know love.

If possible, end the relationship **face-to-face** rather than by text or social media. If this is impossible, write a letter or an email clearly explaining why the relationship is over.

If you are the one finishing the relationship, be **understanding** and **sensitive.** Stop and think about how you would like to be treated in the same situation. Finish things in an honest and respectful way so that the other person feels valued.

> You don't have to be in a relationship to feel happy.

Never allow someone to be your priority while allowing yourself to be their option
Mark Twain

TIPS FOR MOVING ON

It can be really painful when you keep visualising your ex with someone else; worse still is seeing them walking down the street holding hands with your gorgeous next-door neighbour. When you do find out that they are in a new relationship, be **dignified**. Contacting them and lashing out won't make you feel any better. Here are some tips to help you to move on.

✪ It is better to be single than to be in bad relationship. Girls, you do not need a love interest to survive!

✪ We understand that he/she has been an important part of your life, but perhaps you need to accept that the relationship is over. Realise that this chapter of your life has closed and that it is time to move on. Don't cling desperately to a past that is now only a distant memory.

✪ Time helps us to gain perspective. Allow yourself to heal. Constantly being around an ex or contacting them by text or social media is only going to prolong the heartache and misery. Give yourself the space to deal with it all.

✪ Do not bottle-up your emotions. Initially, talking and getting everything off your chest with friends and family is good for you. However, incessantly talking about an ex weeks after is not, so you need to refocus your mind on positive things. Friends get frustrated when you are constantly being negative and, trust us, you will drive them insane every time you mention how wonderful your ex was or how they were the only one who really understood you.

✪ Remember that intense relationships can be hard. Understanding your own emotions and feelings can be difficult enough without trying to deal with someone else's feelings and needs in a close relationship. Your boyfriend/girlfriend may feel overwhelmed by the intensity of the relationship and decide to end it. Do not see this as rejection.

✪ Blame is a negative emotion and serves no positive purpose whatsoever. Blaming your ex, yourself, friends or family is completely pointless. Replaying hurtful scenarios only keeps you focused on the negative. Focus your energy on how to move on and remember that someday you will meet someone who will make you realise why it never worked with anyone else.

✪ Visualisation is a powerful process. Picture yourself being 'over' your ex and looking and feeling fabulous while laughing with your friends. Keep this picture in your mind's eye and it will help to make you feel better. Really! The subconscious mind does not know what is real or imagined, so focus on the positive and, before you know it, you will feel more energised and ready for anything!

✪ Do not go on the rebound in an attempt to try and fill what may feel like a gaping hole. You actually need plenty of time to focus on yourself and nurture your wounded pride before starting a new relationship. Connect with yourself and know that you are wonderful. Boost your self-esteem, which has probably taken a beating since the break-up, by getting a new haircut or a new outfit. Remember: 'Fake it till you make it.'

✪ Sometimes, we view relationships through rose-tinted glasses which can prevent us from seeing if they are as healthy as they should be. Kindness and respect are essential ingredients for any loving relationship.

✪ Going through the heartache and the pain of a break-up helps us to learn to forgive ourselves and others. It makes us stronger and more resilient in the face of challenges. **Some relationships can test us and teach us.** Others bring out the best in us. Don't be afraid to commit to a new, healthy relationship just because old ones didn't work. Every failure is leading to success.

'Sometimes good things fall apart so that better things can fall together.'

✿ Marilyn Monroe ✿

Parent—teen relationships

In order to have a good relationship with your parents, it must be built on respect, trust and understanding. You are dealing with a lot of changes and, at times, you may become preoccupied with your own needs and feelings and forget about everybody else. However, when it comes to having a meaningful relationship with your parents it is important to try to take an interest in each other's lives and make time for one another.

You need to know that you can count on your parents' word and that if they make a promise they will stick to it. Of course it's equally important that you do the same, if you are to gain each other's trust and respect. Your parents may frustrate you, but always remember that you love them. Everyone needs to hear that they are loved. So let your parents know you care about them and make a habit of it.

Try to communicate openly – being isolated in your bedroom and feeling that no one understands you will only add to your problems. Reach out to your parents when you need help or advice: they have lived through adolescence and have learned from their own mistakes. Always remember that they are there to help and guide you and provide you with reliable advice which peers may not yet be able to offer. Your parents don't have a manual on how to deal with every teen issue so be patient with them: they are doing their best and trying to figure it out as they go along.

Remember to have fun – joking together encourages positive relationships. Ask to play an active role in setting boundaries and making rules. Work together. If you give respect, you get it back. It's that simple.

There is no such thing as the perfect family.

Don't be fooled by outward appearances. All families argue and disagree sometimes. Family life teaches you to love and forgive, to accept differences and how to overcome challenges.

Parents fighting

It is upsetting to hear parents yelling at each other, especially if it is frequent and intense. Your stress levels escalate when this happens, so maybe you could put on your headphones and listen to your favourite music to drown out the noise. Then, when things have calmed down, tell your parents how their arguing affects you. It does not have to be a long-winded and difficult conversation. A simple phrase such as 'Please don't fight around me, it stresses me out' can help. If this doesn't work, talk to a favourite teacher in school or an adult you like. Ask for advice and guidance.

Some adults have different parenting styles and this can lead to disagreements. Even if you hear your name mentioned in the row, remember, abusive arguing or domestic violence is never your fault. It is not your job to referee your parents' disagreements.

If you feel that there is a threat of danger to you or anyone in your home, contact the authorities.

Try to stay confident. Do not bury your emotions. Express them in a manner that suits you – whether that's painting a picture, writing poetry in your journal or screaming into a pillow. Most importantly, tell the adults in your life what you are going through.

What if I suspect that one of my parents is drinking too much?

Alcoholism, in one way or another, affects every family in this country. We all know someone who has a drink problem. In Ireland, our attitude to alcohol and drinking in general is a complex one. Living with an alcoholic can be a nightmare for an adult but even worse and more confusing for a teenager. Often, adolescents with an alcoholic parent at home will feel hurt, ashamed, anxious and perhaps, at times, unsafe. Alcoholics are not easy to be around – they are unpredictable at best and toxic at worst. Home may not always feel like the safe haven that it is supposed to be. Some days, everything may seem normal whereas on others all hell may break loose because of the slightest thing. The abnormal can become the norm. Families may find themselves excusing unacceptable and erratic behaviour in an attempt to appease the loved one who is drinking and hoping that by doing so they are making life a little easier for all involved.

Teenagers with an alcoholic mother or father may feel a huge sense of shame, guilt, anger and disappointment towards their parent. If you are living with alcoholism, it is quite possible that you just don't know what to do. You may feel that you are responsible for all the crazy things that are playing out in front of you – you are not. You may be expected to take on the adult role in the house because the actual adults in your life, for whatever reason, are not doing what they are supposed to be doing – that is, loving and caring for you. Living with this problem can be isolating because, the chances are, you are too ashamed to bring your friends back to your house in case your dad is roaring drunk or your mum is falling blindly around the kitchen at four o' clock in the afternoon.

Our advice?

✦ Rally your friends around you. The support and understanding that a good friend can offer can really help you to get through this difficult and confusing time.

✦ Remember that alcoholism is a disease. Your parent is drinking because they are addicted and need, at some stage, to confront their demons and do something about the situation. Do not drive yourself demented trying to change them: you cannot. Only they can change themselves.

✦ Talk to other family members. Decide among you what plans to make and coping strategies to put in place.

✦ Contact Al Anon – they help people living with addictive behaviour. Alternatively, Alateen helps teens who are dealing with alcoholism in the home. These organisations recognise that alcoholism is not just about the alcoholic but the entire family. They know how much suffering and pain is endured by teenagers and they provide real help to deal with the drinking, the emotional abuse, the mood swings and the bewilderment. Both Al Anon and Alateen can help you to understand that alcoholism is a disease just like any other and can, if the person is willing, be cured.

✦ Try not to blame yourself for your parents' drinking. It is important that you realise that it is not your job to 'fix' the problem. Try to protect and love yourself as much as possible. You can remove yourself emotionally and mentally from the chaos – this is called detachment. It doesn't mean that you don't care – it's just a healthier way of coping because, deep down, you know that your happiness and sanity count too.

THINGS WE'D LIKE OUR PARENTS TO KNOW

I never know what to expect when I get home from school – it's like living with lots of different people. Are you going to be your normal self? Aggressive and emotional or downright abusive? It's exhausting.

Let's Talk About Sex

Teens are being bombarded daily with negative media messaging. They are exposed to sex in magazines, film, TV and social media. Boys as young as twelve are becoming addicted to online pornography. Our focus as educators is to teach young adults about sex, contraception, teenage pregnancy and sexually transmitted diseases. However, girls, it is our belief that if you learn from early on to value yourselves then you will be less likely to tolerate undesirable situations and relationships – and be able to say 'No' and mean 'No', if that is how you feel.

Girls often think that if they are sexually desirable they will meet the man of their dreams, i.e. a Theo James lookalike, and live happily ever after. Some feel that they have nothing to give but their bodies. Sadly, they fail to realise that they are worth more than a one-night stand. Because of this they may feel confused, alone, angry and worthless. Peer pressure has a lot to answer for. Girls sometimes believe they will be left on the margins of the group if they do not follow the crowd and do whatever it is their friends are doing. Reality TV shows like *Geordie Shore* or *The Valleys* represent an extremely misguided and often exaggerated version of how young people live. It is important to remember that the legal age of consent in Ireland is seventeen and choosing not to have sex is the perfect and right decision if this is what feels right to you. Chances are you have probably been exposed to disturbing or unusual sexual habits online and you may mistakenly believe that this is the norm. Girls, it is not. While it might seem to you that everyone around you is having sex, remember that lots of teens choose to abstain from sex for many different reasons. If you don't want to have sex, this is your decision. You should own it and be proud of it. Always wait until you feel cherished and respected in your relationship.

These are some of the many comments we have heard down through the years.

✦ *'It's weird and embarrassing to have a conversation about contraception with my boyfriend. I just don't think that I am confident enough in my own skin to talk about this issue.'* Remember: the reality is if you are not comfortable enough to talk about sex and its implications then you probably aren't ready to actually sleep with another person. Never have sex with someone who doesn't respect either you or themselves enough to use protection.

- *'I'm only sixteen. Is it OK not to have sex or how long should I be in a relationship before I have sex?'* Again, remember the legal age of consent is seventeen. Don't let anyone put you under pressure. Take your time; there is nothing wrong with doing things at your own pace. This is a big decision and one not to be taken lightly. Ask yourself: am I ready? Is this what I want? If the honest answer is no, then give yourself whatever length of time you need. What is the rush?

- *'I'm afraid that if I don't have sex with him then he'll end the relationship and break my heart.'* OK, that is a real fear, but we would say that having sex with someone only because you are afraid of losing that person is never a good enough reason to sleep with them. If your boyfriend/girlfriend really loves you, they will not put pressure on you to do something that you are not yet ready for.

In today's world there is massive over-exposure to sex. Oral sex is sometimes, wrongly, accepted as a rite of passage. STIs are infections that are spread from one person to another through close sexual contact, including oral and anal sex. If you are having unprotected sex, visit your doctor or STI clinic for a check-up.

THINGS WE'D LIKE OUR PARENTS TO KNOW

I wish that my parents could understand that when I get dressed up for a night out it's because I want my female friends and members of the opposite sex to think that I look attractive, not because I want to go out and have sex.

Our parents think that if they talk openly with us about sex that they are encouraging us to become more sexually active. The truth is, the more informed we are, the less misinformation we get from friends or other sources. As a result, we are more likely to think twice before jumping into bed with someone.

We appreciate that our parents were teenagers too, so when they discuss relationships and sex in a non-judgemental way and explain their thoughts and beliefs, it helps us to see the logic in resisting the pressure to have sex.

Both boys and girls need to know that their feelings matter and that other people's feelings matter too.

When should you have sex?

Although some teens don't put pressure on each other to have sex, the reality is that in many teenage relationships one person wants to have sex while the other doesn't. One of the toughest decisions a lot of you face is whether to have sex or not. Although you may feel ready physically, sex has serious emotional consequences. Everyone's emotions are different. Just because it is fine for your friends to have sex does not mean that it is the right time for you. This is a significant decision and you must do what is right. You need to know that your partner is with you for the fun, lovely and exciting person you are and not just because they want to sleep with you. If someone is pressurising you into sex they are only thinking about themselves and not considering what matters most to you.

You are responsible for your own body and your own happiness so don't rush into anything.

You have plenty of time to wait until you are ready. A meaningful relationship depends on more than sex. You are powerful enough to make your own decisions, so use your judgement to decide if it is the right time for you to make this huge leap into the adult world. Be certain that your partner is the right person. You will always remember the first time you had sex, so make it a great memory!

Questions to ask yourself before having sex

+ Do I love this person?

+ Do they love me?

+ Do they respect me?

+ Can I trust my partner?

+ Do I feel ready and comfortable with myself and my partner to have sex?

+ Am I doing this because I really want to or am I just trying to keep them happy?

+ What are my reasons for having sex?

+ What do I think is going to happen after we've had sex? Will they stay with me or just move on?

+ Does the person I am going to have sex with want to have sex with me or just want to have sex?

+ Can I talk comfortably with them about sex, pregnancy and STIs? If not, why not?

+ Is my decision to have sex based on the right reasons?

'Sex is hardly ever just about sex.'

Shirley MacLaine

Kissing

While some girls feel pressure to have sex, others say they feel extremely anxious when they are pressurised by friends to kiss someone for the first time. Our words of advice – go easy on yourself and do not expect perfection!

You may have seen lots of 'perfect' kisses in romantic movies, but remember that in real life kisses only become fantastic with practice. Nobody really knows what they are doing at first. Don't be afraid that you will be bad at kissing. If you are petrified because it is your first kiss and you don't want to mess up, relax. The person lucky enough to be kissing you will never know that it is your first time. Let the other person lead. Relax, slow down and enjoy the experience! Remember, there is more than one way to kiss, so you won't get it wrong.

Teenage pregnancy

It is very possible that you are feeling confused, shocked and frightened if you have just learned that you are pregnant. You are probably building up the courage to tell the baby's father and it is understandable that you are wondering how you are going to tell your parents, not to mention his. Everyone reacts differently. You know your parents. Some parents scream and yell, some are emotional and cry, others go into shock and denial and don't show how they feel at first, while there are those who spring into action, trying to take charge and control the situation. If you are afraid that your parents may react violently to the news, ensure that someone like a family friend or a relative is there to keep things as calm as possible.

It can be hard to know exactly what to say but something as simple as 'I have something difficult to tell you and I know this isn't what you wanted for me but … I'm pregnant' may work for you.

The key is to be honest. Give your parents time to speak without interrupting them. Share your deepest fears and worries. Say things like 'I am scared about how I am going to handle this.' Some families need the help of a counsellor to work through difficult and complicated issues such as keeping the baby or letting someone else adopt the child. This allows everyone's opinion to be heard and respected.

How you feel often depends on how much support you have from your family, the baby's father and friends. There may be days when you feel sad and confused while at other times you could be feeling excited and happy. It is natural to wonder whether you are ready to handle the responsibilities that come with being a parent. Talk to your parents whenever you can to help you process your feelings and any issues that may crop up. If your family are unsupportive, enlist the help of friends or any other supportive adult. Never be afraid to reach out.

Take good care of yourself so that you and your baby will be healthy. Smoking, taking drugs and drinking alcohol cause all sorts of problems and put you and your baby at risk, so avoid them at all costs. Healthy foods and plenty of water will help your developing baby to thrive. There are certain foods such as unpasteurised cheese and shellfish that need to be avoided during pregnancy so make sure to talk to your doctor about this. Find out what supplements you may need to take. Ask your doctor about the physical and emotional changes you will experience during pregnancy. Read books, attend classes and check out reputable websites to learn more about what to expect when it comes to becoming a parent and raising a child.

Remember, you are never alone. Reach out.

Alcohol, rape and sexual abuse

Alcohol

Alcohol features largely in teens' lives. Many of your peers experiment with alcohol out of curiosity and in order to fit in. Remember, though – in Ireland you must be over 18 years of age to purchase alcoholic drinks or be on the premises of a public house or retailer without the company of an adult. Be careful around alcohol. It makes you feel less inhibited, so it is quite likely that you will feel happier and more popular as well as much more confident. However, after a few drinks your ability to make decisions and stay in control is affected and you could end up doing foolish , not to mention embarrassing, things. Alcohol is also a depressant, which may cause you to feel sad or angry. Also, drinking in public places, such as fields, parks and streets is illegal for minors and could result in alcohol being confiscated and parents or guardians being contacted. Here are some things you should consider when thinking about alcohol and drinking.

✦ You really don't want to be the girl who is falling around the night club. During your teens the human brain is still developing so drinking excessively can affect your behaviour and also damage your ability to get good grades and study productively.

✦ If you want to enjoy a drink, know your limits and stick to them. Many students tell us about the frustration they feel when they have to look after drunken friends. Drink sensibly. Don't be the one who ruins everyone's night out.

✦ Some teenagers have told us how they go 'creeping' when there is a disco on that they are not going to, in order to see what friends are wearing and, more importantly, what they are getting up to! They say that when they actually stand back and look impartially and soberly at friends who are teetering in high heels and wearing very short dresses, they realise how ridiculous it all can be.

✦ Don't let peers pressurise you into drinking more than you plan to.

✦ Drink slowly. Pace your drinking and add lots of mixers to your drinks to make them last longer.

✦ Drink plenty of water on a night out to keep your body hydrated as alcohol dehydrates.

✦ Don't drink on an empty stomach.

✦ When it comes to drugs, you may feel that you are immune to others' problems and experiences. You don't want to harm yourself and others. Drugs are addictive and drug use is linked with a range of negative consequences such as school failure, unsafe sex, addiction, mental health issues and suicide. Stop and realise that today's actions have a huge impact on your future. **JUST. SAY. NO.**

✦ According to the Rape and Justice in Ireland (RAJI) study, the majority of rape cases in Ireland (80 per cent) involve a perpetrator and a victim who have consumed alcohol. The RAJI study found that in 10 per cent of rape cases the complainant was completely incapacitated and it was generally an acquaintance or friend who committed the rape.

Maybe it is time that we all took a serious look at alcohol consumption in Ireland. 'Bingeing' with friends where you intentionally go out to get obliterated is dangerous.

> Look after yourself like you would look after a little sister or a really close friend. You deserve to be safe.

Rape and sexual abuse

Rape is defined in the Criminal Law (Rape) Act 1987 as 'unlawful sexual intercourse with a woman who at the time of the incident does not consent to it' where the man 'knows that she **does not consent** … or he is reckless as to whether she does or does not consent to it.' Rape under section 4 of the Criminal Law (Rape) (Amendment) Act 1990 applies to attacks on both men and women.

Aggravated sexual assault is a sexual attack that involves serious violence or causes grave injury, humiliation or degradation to the victim.

Sexual assault is a sexual attack with a less serious level of violence.

Irishhealth.com says, 'sexual abuse can be physical or emotional and involves tricking, bribing, forcing or pressurising a child or teenager into sexual awareness or activity. Sexual abuse involves the use of a child or teenager by an older or more knowledgeable person for their own sexual pleasure. It often begins gradually and increases insidiously over time.'

Rape, assault and abuse are distressing and frightening topics. If you are drunk or high you may not be conscious of someone slipping a date-rape drug such as Rohypnol into your drink. When you are on a night out keep your drink with you at all times. When you are under the influence you are more likely to do something which you would never otherwise do, like get into a dangerous situation or go off on your own with a stranger. Our tip – always stay with your friends on a night out. Remember, girls, there really is safety in numbers.

After an assault, some girls blame themselves for the terrible thing that has happened to them. They mistakenly think that somehow the attack was their fault, citing what they wore and things they said as reasons for what happened. The perpetrator is the one who is responsible for the attack and not the victim.

At times, the road to healing may seem like a gruelling and somewhat terrifying one. Confusion, shock, fear, anger and denial are all very normal feelings and emotions. While the experience is devastating, there is hope when you decide to choose a healing path. Saying nothing doesn't help you to deal with the pain. Breaking the silence and asking for help may seem like the most difficult thing you'll ever have to do. However, it is often the first step towards recovery.

'I am not what happened to me.
I am what I choose to become.'

Carl Jung

If someone you know has decided to confide in you about being raped, assaulted or abused, it is imperative that they feel safe and know that you believe them. It is a distressing disclosure and you may feel powerless when faced with your friend's pain and confusion. Your sense of grief for them may consume you. Listen without interrupting with your own emotions and suggestions. Acknowledge their feelings about what has happened. Tell them how strong and courageous they are to have survived this trauma and to be able to speak out about it. Do not put pressure on yourself; you do not have all the answers. Encourage your friend to seek support.

If you have been a victim of rape or sexual abuse, it can be helpful to talk to a counsellor who could help you to clarify your emotions and feelings surrounding the abuse. Counsellors who integrate expressive therapies such as art therapy, music therapy or dance therapy can be very effective for teenagers. After contacting your local crisis centre, you might wish to join a support group. Talking to other survivors helps. You may feel like you have a mountain to climb, but starting on the road to healing helps the mountain to seem smaller until finally it begins to erode. Gradually, through talking and with therapy, you will discover that the trauma does not define you.

Stay moving forward: you can reclaim your life.

Mean Girls

(S) Watching *The Late Late Show* in May 2015, I was incredibly impressed by a young man from Dublin who had been the victim of an intense cyberbullying campaign. He revealed to Ryan Tubridy and the audience how distressed he had felt when he discovered that a photograph of him posted online had become the source of people's amusement. He urged teenagers to think twice before they 'like' something on Facebook, saying that this one post had torn his life in two. The worst part of the entire experience, according to him, was that the bullying was anonymous. Towards the end of the interview, Ryan asked him what he was going to do when he left school. He modestly replied that he had been offered a place in Oxford to study law. I have to say that this impressive teenager made me sit up and take notice – here was someone who had not only survived bullying but was also now on his way to bigger and more fantastic things. You have got to love a story with a happy ending ...

(M) Over the years, I have been a class tutor many times. This role is not an academic one but pastoral. In other words, it is the tutor's job to keep an eagle eye on the students sitting in front of them. If there are problems at home or sickness in the family, the tutor is usually one of the first to know. My students have often said that a good tutor should almost be like, and I quote, 'a mammy in school'. I love the job, as you really get to know your students over a two- or three-year period and it can be deeply fulfilling. However, every now and then bullying crops up ...

Bullying is the single most difficult aspect of school life to deal with. Why? Well, for starters, it can be notoriously difficult to detect. Students can be sitting in front of you for quite some time before the cracks in their armour begin to appear. Girls especially are great actors! They can smile sweetly up at you when, in reality, they are planning their next attack on some vulnerable girl in the classroom. The victims are often too mortified to say anything to anybody, especially a teacher, in case they draw more shame on themselves. And we use the word 'shame' deliberately here. The victims of bullying almost always feel that they are somehow responsible for the relentless attacks that they receive on a daily basis in school. Of course, these days they cannot escape from the torture when they walk out of the school gates. The insults and abuse continue in the form of bitchy texts and malicious posts online. These anonymous comments can have a devastating impact on young people's self-confidence. Worse still is when you do not know who is writing such awful things about you. Technology has afforded teens the chance to take bullying, which once existed only in school hallways, into cyberspace.

Never feel ashamed about being the victim of bullying – it is not your fault.

Girls often use emotional abuse or emotional violence when they wish to bully someone in their peer group. This alienating and malicious behaviour leaves their victims feeling lonely and miserable. We have known girls to gang up on or exclude peers – they do this for many reasons but, in our experience, jealousy is the main one.

(S) I remember a girl who was forever being pushed out of the group for no other reason than she was absolutely stunning and more intelligent than the whole group put together. She didn't know or understand what was happening to her, but after a little investigation, it became very evident that she intimidated her group and made them feel inferior. They used to whisper things to each other in her company, making her feel foolish and completely left out. Girls know instinctively how to press each other's buttons and sometimes do so to devastating effect.

What is bullying?

Bullying is a very real problem. It occurs when someone intentionally sets out to target someone else. It can happen in schools, in the workplace, online and even at home. It is a distressing experience and one which no one should have to go through on their own. There are many different types of bullying, including physical, verbal and emotional. Girls have a tendency to alienate or exclude classmates, which can be very hurtful, not to mention confusing, for the person left on the fringes. At other times, they can harass their peers, repeatedly demeaning them, spreading rumours about them or constantly making them feel inadequate or belittled. Girls tend to be very subtle when it comes to bullying. It can just take one sarcastic remark to make someone feel like their world is collapsing. Over the years, many parents have told us how their child has been suddenly and often brutally excluded from the group for no apparent reason. When this happens, the person who is being left out in the cold is often at a complete loss about what they should do and how to resolve it.

It is easier to notice the student who is being bullied first. Finding out who is doing the bullying can be far more difficult, as students can close ranks. Often, concerned friends or even **a student with integrity and strength of character** will come up to us privately and confess that they don't like what is playing out in their classroom. It is then the teacher's job to take action and talk to the student being bullied first. Not in the classroom where all eyes are on her, but somewhere more private. The victim will often deny that anything untoward is going on. But, and this is the good news, keeping up this show of strength often proves too much and eventually the mask slips and the teen expresses her distress at what is going on. If this all sounds easy, trust us, it's not. It can take a long time to get to this point.

Often at this stage, girls being bullied will confess that they did nothing to improve their situation because they just hoped that it would go away of its own accord. Now, sometimes this can happen, but more often than not this is not the case. They will say that what is happening to them is not really bullying but harmless teasing. They often think that they need to grow a thicker skin and get on with things. But when does teasing become bullying? It is when you frequently walk away from encounters feeling belittled and powerless. You know that if you are feeling in your heart like something is wrong, then it probably is. Students need to trust themselves. Listen to your inner voice. If you don't feel right, then you know that something is wrong.

> Your life matters, you deserve to be free from fear and really live.

Why me?

It can be hard to accept that you are the one being bullied. Girls often ask themselves (and rightly so) why me? What have I done to deserve this? Sometimes, it can be the simplest thing – for example, you got full marks in your History test and your 'friend' flunked again. It could be down to boy trouble – maybe the boy she worships has his eye on you instead and she wants to lash out. It seems that most bullying among girls tends to be about boys. Of course it could be none of the above and you are just an easy target in her eyes because you are more reserved than she is. It doesn't have to be anything specific. What is important here is that you can take back control of your life today. Many teenagers initially fear that there will be further bullying if adults become involved. This is not the case. If you don't do anything about it, your problems will only intensify. Talk to somebody you love or someone you know that you can trust. Confide in them, decide that enough is enough and begin to rally back.

What about the bullies?

'I would rather be a little nobody, than to be an evil somebody.'

Abraham Lincoln

(M) I remember the first time I dealt with bullying in a girls school. I was naive and inexperienced and my heart went out to the junior student who, at thirteen, was being bullied mercilessly by another girl who was older than her. She would meet this senior student on the corridors at lunchtime. The bully would push the younger student around and throw her lunch to the ground while the bully's entourage laughed and sneered. This is predictable bullying behaviour. As I was the tutor of the junior student, it was my job to do something about it. I remember talking to an older member of staff who had years of experience under her belt, saying how I had no sympathy for the bully who, in my view, deserved no pity. My colleague disagreed wholeheartedly, reminding me that the bully was a victim also and she was simply lashing out in a desperate bid for attention. If you are suffering at the hands of a school bully it can be very difficult to see them in this forgiving light. However, it is necessary to look at this issue from both perspectives if you are to come through this difficult period with a feeling of closure, healing and understanding.

Girls bully because they are feeling pain, hurt or rejection at a very deep level. A happy person would never inflict pain or suffering on another. In fact, the thought wouldn't even cross their mind. Bullies often do not even recognise this and it can take time for them to open up and admit that something is wrong in their life – or sometimes they don't even realise that they are bullying at all. They bully other students because the act itself gives them a feeling of control and power. Other areas of their life may be slipping out of their control and often there is trouble at home. Exerting power over others and humiliating them gives them a sense of control temporarily. However, **being a bully brings more pain.** It's like a boomerang: what you send out comes back and often the bullies will admit that hurting another student actually makes them feel even worse about themselves.

If you are a bystander when bullying is occurring in front of you, and laughing when someone is being victimised, this is an indirect way of bullying.

It sends out the message that you approve of this behaviour. Be responsible and report it anonymously. Remember, nobody has the right to take away another person's dignity and make their life a misery.

How can I stop being a bully?

Changing a habit such as bullying can take time and patience, but it is possible. Maybe you are not feeling particularly good about yourself. Try to figure out the reasons behind your actions. Confront what is causing you to bully people. You might be fooled into thinking that you are popular among your peers because they laugh at your aggressive behaviour, but the truth is they are probably afraid of you. Take a long, hard and honest look at yourself and ask 'Is this really who I want to be?' Deep down, you probably recognise that your behaviour is wrong. It is **never** OK to hurt another person. Everyone deserves to be treated equally and with fairness. Decide to make a new start. **Apologise for your behaviour, even if it's the hardest thing that you have ever done.** Find other ways of dealing with your anger. Develop new interests and try to make positive friendships. It is never too late to change for the better. So do it today.

'It's never too late – never too late to start over, never too late to be happy.'

×♡ Jane Fonda ♡×

Bullying because of race can be particularly distressing as it isolates the teen from their peer group and it is very hard for the teen to counteract, as it directly attacks their self-confidence. It can involve intentionally hurtful remarks or physical attacks on someone because of the colour of their skin, their nationality or their cultural or religious practices. We are all different. Everyone has a right to be treated fairly and with respect. No one deserves to be a victim of bullying. Thankfully, more support is being put in place to prevent racist bullying, but one form of bullying that is still not addressed enough is homophobic bullying.

Homophobic bullying

Becoming a teenager involves coming to grips with one's identity. Relationships are an obvious part of growing up and can cause problems of their own. How difficult is it then if a teenager feels that they may be gay, lesbian, transgender or bisexual? As a society, we are now far more accepting about people's sexual orientation but this acceptance doesn't always extend to the classroom. As educators, teachers have an important role in easing the pressure and uncertainty for teens who are questioning their sexual orientation. Depending on who you listen to, between 8 per cent and 11 per cent of the population are homosexual. That means that for every class of thirty students sitting in front of us, statistically, three could be gay. Yet how often are the voices of these students left unheard?

Belong To is a group which has recently launched a pilot programme in schools. Its aim is to educate young people about gay rights and inclusivity. Language is powerful; perhaps it's time to examine some of the words and phrases which we use daily. Derogatory language needs to be challenged. How often have you used the term 'that's so gay' without really thinking of its implications? Every student should feel safe in school.

Coming out can be one of the hardest things for a teenager to do, as they may be terrified of the reaction they will get. The thought of telling parents and friends can be very stressful. Fear of rejection from their parents and friends and bullying and harassment are a real concern. Rejection from a parent is any teen's worst nightmare. Bullying, also, makes a difficult situation appear almost unbearable.

TIP

- ✪ If you are still figuring out your sexual orientation, be careful who you talk to. Tell someone you really trust.

- ✪ Give yourself the gift of time to figure out how you really feel. Let your parents know what is going on. **They love you and will want to help.**

THINGS WE'D LIKE OUR PARENTS TO KNOW

Listen to what I have to say in a non-judgemental manner. All I want is for you to be there for me.

Remember, coming out is a very brave thing to do and it will impact hugely on many aspects of your life. Don't be too upset if some friends distance themselves from you or begin to gradually drift away. Remind yourself that people who do this were not true friends to begin with. You cannot force anyone to be tolerant. However, on the flip-side your true friends will always cherish you, support you and defend you. They will always respect and love you exactly the way you are. So if times are challenging at the moment, hold on to that thought.

Cyberbullying

Bullying twenty years ago was bad enough when you had to go through an entire school day waiting for the dreaded bullies to pounce. Now it's much worse, as the abuse can go on 24/7 thanks to smartphones and tablets. Here are some startling statistics which make for worrying reading.

✳ Nearly 43 per cent of students **have** been bullied online.

✳ Over 80 per cent of teenagers use a mobile phone regularly, making it the most common medium for cyberbullying.

✳ 68 per cent of teens agree that cyberbullying is a serious problem. (DoSomething.org)

Cyberbullying happens for the same reasons as regular bullying but the advantages to this form of bullying, from the bully's point of view, is that it is **completely anonymous**. They do not have to take ownership or responsibility for posting images or comments online which are deliberately intended to hurt and degrade someone else. Stopbullying.gov pinpoints two types of teenagers who are most likely to bully their peers online. They are students who perceive themselves as the popular ones and those who are on the margins. Again, cyberbullying makes those perpetuating the misery feel more powerful. For students who are ignored, invisible and always on the edge of what is going on, cyberbullying can help with their feelings of low self-worth. This form of bullying takes little courage so is often attractive for teens who have self-esteem issues. Also, many don't realise or even care about the consequences because **they don't see how their comments hurt their victims in person**: they don't fully process the damage that they are inflicting. Actually, it is their very insecurities and hang-ups that make the bullies want to inflict as much pain as possible on somebody else. You may not view yourself as a bully, but ask yourself how often have you 'liked' a post online without even looking at it properly? Take ownership of your online activities. Think before you do anything you might later regret.

About two years ago we had an in-service training programme about teacher–student relationships. The facilitator was excellent – he was funny and informative. He told us that teenagers don't fully develop empathy until their late teens and even early twenties. This fact surprised us at the time but it is relevant here. Some may engage in the practice of cyber-bullying and think it is perfectly acceptable to do so, especially if all of their friends are encouraging them.

What can be done to stop cyberbullying?

Recently in class we were discussing technology. The subject of cyberbullying was broached and the girls were asked how serious it was. Here are some of their replies.

✦ 'It's a major issue. Everyone is being judged somehow.'

✦ 'This is a problem which needs to be acted on and dealt with.'

✦ 'Cyberbullying is worrying! I mainly see it on Facebook. I am often disturbed and surprised at who is doing the bullying. Recently, I saw that a senior student was mocking a fourteen-year-old. That's not right.'

✦ 'It is an issue. People have a right to be happy online.'

- ✦ 'This seems to be an issue with younger students, I mean, twelve–fifteen-year-olds. Boys and girls are comparing themselves on social media sites. Incriminating photos are being taken at school discos and posted for the whole world to see. It's tough out there.'

- ✦ 'This is a huge issue and it's not being tackled.'

- ✦ 'You can't escape even after you have finished a hard day at school – you can still be bullied online when you get home.'

We can all help to stamp out cyberbullying. Teens need to be taught that is never acceptable and that it can cause long-term problems for those involved. Think about your posts and who you send them to. Ask yourself, would I be happy if someone posted this about me? If the answer is 'No', don't send it.

TIPS

- ✪ If you receive an abusive or spiteful message online, do not bother to respond. Instead, save it or print it so that you can show it to an adult you trust at a later stage.

- ✪ It is **never** wise to give your personal information out to strangers online.

- ✪ Do not tell anyone except your parents what your password is. Do not give this information to your friends.

- ✪ **Be the same person online as you are in real life.** That means don't write anything online that you wouldn't be prepared to say to a person face-to-face.

- ✪ Avoid websites which rate teens as smartest, prettiest, ugliest or fattest.

- ✪ Do not let people trick you into revealing personal or humiliating information – they may then send this to others.

- ✪ Remember, you do not need to tell the world **everything** about your life. **Privacy** is underrated in today's world.

Asking for help

If you are being bullied, talk to someone about it today. Do not tell yourself that it will all blow over in a few weeks or months; the longer you leave this problem, the worse it can get. Enlist help from people who have your best interests at heart. Remember, it can be sorted; you have to be brave and take a leap of faith. And lastly, and probably most importantly, just because this is happening to you right now, don't lose sight of the wonderful, attractive, loveable human being that you are. Do not give up on yourself. Focus on your strengths and take back control from the people who are doing this to you. Do it today.

Remember: You can and will get through this.

Love Your Curves

Body image is how we see, think and feel about the way we look and how we think others perceive us. It can be influenced by attitudes and beliefs as well as peer groups, society and the media. When it comes to your shape and appearance, try to remember that we are all different. Learn to accept this diversity.

Beauty is a state of mind – not a look.

The definition of the 'perfect' body type is constantly changing. Many of you develop your body image in accordance with ideas advanced by the media. Advertisements seduce us with the promise that if we buy the right products and stay on trend then we too can be attractive. They scream at us from our TV screens that we are worth it. Worth what exactly? Many of us are brainwashed into believing that beautiful people are happier, richer, smarter and more popular than other mere mortals. Do you sometimes feel the need to strive for perfection and then wonder why you are left feeling like you don't quite measure up? When you feel this way for a long time, low self-esteem can become a real issue and the pressure to live up to unattainable ideals can have a negative effect on how you view your body and, ultimately, yourself.

Let's face it: even Keira Knightley has flaws. Why not learn to accept yours and view them as 'perfect imperfections'? They make us unique. It is not just our physical appearance that shows our beauty, but also our ability to love and embrace our physical uniqueness.

We say, redefine your interpretation of beauty – don't worry whether it fits society's standards or not. Instead, identify and work to your strengths. You, and you alone, have the ability and power to improve your self-esteem. Since when did 'the way I look' become the most important measure of self-worth? Discover the beauty in your imperfections today, girls, and know that you are gorgeous!

Having a healthy body image does not mean that you think your body is wonderful and that you are perfect beyond belief. It just means that you are comfortable with the body that you inhabit and are committed to caring for it as best you can by eating healthy food and exercising.

> 'You wouldn't worry so much about what others think of you if you realised how seldom they do.'
>
> Eleanor Roosevelt

As girls move through adolescence each blemish and pimple, as well as every pound gained, can be traumatic. What we don't realise at the time is that everything that occurs during adolescence is a stage – you're making a short pit-stop on the road to adulthood. Things don't last forever. What happens during puberty can influence how some individuals feel about themselves long into the future, so try to accept that the changes are temporary ones.

Develop a healthy scepticism about what is 'real'

In a *Daily Mail* interview Rihanna said:

> 'You shouldn't be pressured into trying to be thin by the fashion industry because they only want models that are like human mannequins. But you have to remember that it's not practical or possible for an everyday woman to be like that. Being size zero is a career in itself so we shouldn't try and be like them. It's not realistic and it's not healthy.'

Celebrity culture is pushed down our throats, especially now with social media and the constant connectivity of the world. Every day, we are exposed to media images which are airbrushed and enhanced as people feel the need to Instagram every moment of their lives.

Photo-manipulation and stylists, not to mention cosmetic surgery, create what **we think** are realities. These distorted or filtered images place pressure on us to attain perfection – or, rather, the fashion industry's idea of perfection. These fabrications manipulate us and make us think that we are too fat, too skinny, too short or too tall or, horror of horrors, too ordinary.

'If you look for perfection, you will never be content.'
Leo Tolstoy

Extreme diets don't work!

Dieting during adolescence can be dangerous. Girls who are constantly hungry and obsessing about calories and every single morsel which passes their lips may become depressed and lose interest in their friends, hobbies and life in general. In extreme cases, they can develop body-image or eating disorders and may need the support of a professional who can help them to develop a healthy body image and provide positive feedback and advice about the way forward. So if you are concerned about your weight talk to your parents, your doctor or another trusted adult.

Self-esteem and body image

Some of the ideas below should make it easier for you to accept who you really are. **Getting other people to like you will never be a substitute for liking yourself.** All bodies are unique.

> You cannot become someone else,
> so why not learn to love, accept and embrace
> whatever it is that makes you different?

THINGS WE'D LIKE OUR PARENTS TO KNOW

If we hear you talking about weight then we become more conscious of it. If you talk negatively about your body then we learn to be negative about ours. We'd love you to talk about being healthy rather than being skinny.

It's not good when you criticise other women in magazines or ask 'Who does she think she is?' when you see a woman on TV who is confident and sassy and has the courage to believe in herself. When you do this, I sometimes think that I can only find the positive in myself when I am belittling others.

When you are trying on clothes or looking in the mirror and saying things like 'This looks terrible on me', my brain fills with negative self-talk. Fashion and make-up can make people miserable but they can also be a fantastic way to express yourself. I know that it takes a strong sense of self to navigate the world of beauty on your own terms. Please help me to approach it with a sense of joy and excitement and not dread and apprehension.

TIPS TO SHINE!

When you wake in the morning, look in the mirror and write three compliments about yourself in your journal. Keep a list of things that you like about yourself that have nothing to do with your body. Read them **all** the time. Here are some phrases you could use to get you started.

- 'I am starting to accept myself more and more.'
- 'I like … about myself.' (Insert your own compliments here.)

✪ Negative self-talk is discouraging and leaves us feeling awful. Saying things like 'I'm so fat' and 'I have horrible skin' do nothing to make us feel better about ourselves and need to be monitored and challenged. On the other hand, positive self-talk makes us believe that we can shoot for the stars and do anything. Say nice things to yourself like 'I'm really working on reaching a healthy body weight: I can do this!' or 'My skin is improving all the time' or 'When I wear clothes I feel comfortable in, I feel happy and confident.'

✪ Visualisations can be very effective. Perhaps your goal is healthy eating and exercising every second day. Imagine the future as if your fairy godmother has waved her magic wand; see yourself looking fit, fab and amazing. Picture the scene in as much detail as possible. Concentrate on it for at least five minutes every night, just before you nod off, or in the morning when you open your eyes.

✪ As much as you can, try to eat well and exercise. Keeping active ensures that your body stays healthy and you feel energised and happy. Drink water regularly throughout the day, about two litres in total. If you wish, you can add a squeeze of lemon or orange for flavour. Appreciate your body for what it is capable of doing and thank it every morning for looking after you so well.

✪ There are nice ways of saying everything. If someone has a weight problem, you can be sure that they are aware of it. Remember that weight is just a number and it can change. Negative remarks serve no purpose and only make people feel more disheartened and could even escalate a problem.

✪ Try to wear clothes that are comfortable and make you feel confident about your body. Dress to suit your shape. Not every trend is right for you.

✪ Be nice to yourself and others. Taking the time to be pleasant makes you feel better about yourself.

✪ Talk to your friends about body confidence and you will soon realise that everyone cares, worries and, yes, even obsesses about the way they look. You might think that your friend is perfect in every way only to realise that she is conscious of how small her bust is or worried that she is too skinny.

✪ Posture is important so learn to walk with a sense of confidence. Walking into a room with your head held high, maintaining eye contact and giving a firm handshake makes you instantly more attractive. People will notice! Accept yourself, love yourself. Celebrate being you. Everyone else is taken!

'For beautiful eyes, look for the good in others;
for beautiful lips, speak only words of kindness;
and for poise, walk with the knowledge
that you are never alone.'

Audrey Hepburn

Body Shape

We all want to feel connected with those around us. It can be frustrating when we think our friends look amazing and we don't. The key to looking good is confidence. If you have confidence and feel happy about yourself you will look great. Women come in all different shapes and sizes. You could be long and lean, curvy or rounded. Instead of criticising your 'wide' hips, 'big' legs, 'fat' arms or 'enormous' backside, learn to accept that you can look amazing no matter what. It's all down to attitude, girls.

Clothes are more than just pieces of material. When clothes are **too small or too tight you feel uncomfortable**, as they will dig into the body, pucker and sit incorrectly. What suits the most popular girl in class may not necessarily suit you. Body shape is all about **proportion**, and style is all about dressing those proportions.

> **I accept my body shape and acknowledge that I am beautiful.**

Clothes and colour can sometimes play a big part in accentuating your best assets, and feeling comfortable in your clothes makes all the features you previously viewed as flaws easier to accept. Having self-confidence is the icing on the cake and the whole point here is to change your negative perceptions and feel good about yourself. In this way your confidence, self-image and self-esteem will sky-rocket!

> **You are beautiful! Believe it.**

Let's Get Physical

Superfoods ... supermodels ... supersize ... size zero ... vegans... vegetarians ... When did eating get so complicated! Your life moves at a break-neck pace and sometimes it can feel like it's hard to keep up, between juggling school, romance, activities, family and friends. Some nights you might be so exhausted and bleary eyed that the only thing you have the energy to eat is a hasty pot noodle or a takeaway pizza in front of the TV. While fast food is perfectly fine every now and then, you know that, long-term, it is not a healthy option. So what do you do if, like the rest of us, you just want to be healthy but don't want to turn into a fanatic who jogs 10k before breakfast, lives on wheatgrass shots and would rather die than eat a large packet of Maltesers? A healthy diet does not mean giving up on all your favourite foods. It may require some effort to change your eating habits, but even a few simple changes can make all the difference.

Food, hygiene and exercise

Nowadays, as we are constantly bombarded with images of perfect bodies on TV and the Internet, it's difficult not to be extremely aware of our bodies and conscious about our weight. Programmes like *Operation Transformation* show us how being obese or overweight can affect self-esteem and may increase the risk of certain health conditions such as heart disease and type-2 diabetes. A healthy, varied diet is essential to ensure that we receive all the nutrients and energy we need. Eating well helps us to concentrate better in school, focus more clearly on daily tasks, participate in extra-curricular activities and maintain a healthy weight and attitude towards food.

'Beauty is being the best possible version of you on the inside and out.'

Anonymous

Be good to your body and be grateful for how amazing it is.

71

TIPS FOR HEALTHY LIVING

✪ **Breakfast is important. Do not skip it!** Starting with a good breakfast will help you to concentrate during the day and increase your attention span.

✪ Skipping meals is never a good idea because it can lead to snacking on unhealthy alternatives. Eat three meals a day: breakfast, lunch and dinner. Try to ensure that each meal includes at least one serving of fruit or vegetables, which are not only delicious but contain fibre, minerals and vitamins. Eat starchy foods such as wholemeal bread, wholemeal pasta or potatoes, which will help to fill you up and give you energy and vitality. Helping with the cooking at home might even inspire you to create healthy meals yourself. So why not don the apron and get creative? Who knows – you could become the next Rachel or Jamie!

✪ It takes twenty minutes for your brain to send a message to your stomach that it is full. Eat more slowly.

✪ Make sure that you eat at least five portions of fruit and vegetables every day. A portion is 80g.

✪ Instead of buying junk food from vending machines, try packing your lunch with healthy options such as lean turkey, wholegrain sandwiches, fruit, nuts and yogurt.

✪ Drink plenty of fluids, particularly water, to prevent the body from dehydrating.

✪ Calcium is also very important as it is needed for the formation and maintenance of strong bones and teeth. It is also vital for the proper functioning of nerves and muscles.

✪ Try to reduce foods that are high in sugar, salt, fat and saturates, such as sweets, chocolates, cakes, fried chips and fried snacks.

✪ **Look after your teeth.** Gum disease has been linked to a lot of health problems in different parts of the body. Brushing and flossing your teeth helps to prevent gum disease.

- When your body starts to change, sweat glands become much more active. This is particularly true for glands in the armpits, groin, on the soles of the feet and on the palms of the hands. An odour is produced when sweat comes in contact with bacteria on the skin. This odour can be stronger in some people than others, so it is very important to shower regularly. Cleanliness is not just important for your health, but it's also necessary to function socially. You do not want to be the student that everyone avoids in class because you couldn't be bothered to shower. Get up earlier in the morning and start the day feeling good about yourself.

- Ask a friend, a parent or a sibling to try healthier eating with you. Relapses can happen so don't quit. If you fail, do not give up; find the strength to try again the next day.

- The brain is a fatty organ – over 60 per cent of it is made up of fats. One-third of this fat is called omega-3, which is essential for hormones, memory and moods. Try to eat oily fish three times per week or take a good-quality fish oil supplement if you can't manage this.

- Exercise helps to use up oxygen; it causes our body to burn stored fat and helps us to maintain a normal weight. Being physically active does not mean that you have to join a gym or play a competitive sport, but if you don't like to exercise alone, joining a team or a club can really help. So turn the televisions and computers off and give it a go. At lunchtime chatting with friends is important, so why not combine the two and go for a 'walk and talk'? Keeping active will make you stronger physically and mentally.

'All truly good thoughts are conceived while walking.'
Friedrich Nietzsche

Skincare

Spots, pimples and acne are the number one enemy of every teen. According to irishhealth.com, eight out of ten adolescents will experience some degree of acne during the teenage years. Spots can bring you down and even leave you feeling depressed. Sometimes, you might feel like the only girl in the world who hasn't been blessed with perfect skin.

'My spots really affect my confidence; they even change how I feel about myself!' How many times have we heard this? We genuinely understand but would urge you not to hide away. Instead, try to be brave and never be afraid to look the world straight in the eye. Everyone has imperfections – instead of only focusing on your spots, turn your attention to your sparkling eyes or your amazing smile. Zone in on the positive and keep telling yourself that, sooner or later, those spots will go! Remind yourself that most of the time people are only thinking about how **they** look, what they are going to say or do next and how others perceive them. They are actually far too worried about themselves to give much thought to you or any flaws that you perceive to be yours. If you confidently look someone in the eye when you are talking to them and listen to what they have to say, they will remember the conversation you had and not the spots on your forehead.

Having said this, we know acne can halt you in your tracks, so here are a few things that you can do to take control of the situation and shine your way through! Remember, everyone's skin is unique and different and what works for one person may not necessarily work for another. However, it's still a good idea to incorporate these tips into your skincare regime.

TIPS FOR HEALTHY SKIN

- ✪ Drink plenty of water to flush out toxins. Think about how the water level in a vase of flowers diminishes gradually. This also happens to our skin so we need to keep it hydrated. Water regulates body temperature, aids in the absorption and digestion of food, carries nutrients to the skin and takes waste away from our cells.

- ✪ We breathe all the time and we tend to take it for granted. We rarely stop to consider what a vital process it is. Breathing exercises make your skin glow, as breathing oxygenates your skin, making it look alive, vibrant and gorgeous.

- Thorough cleansing is essential: use a creamy cleanser and wipe it off with a face cloth in warm water in order to remove surface oils and dead skin cells. Aim to wash your face at least twice a day. The skin must be treated gently so do not go overboard on products; try to keep them as natural as possible. Scrubbing your skin aggressively with an abrasive cleanser can be very harmful and can even further irritate the skin.

- Prolonged exposure to exam anxiety increases stress hormones which in turn creates oxidative stress. To combat this, eat fruit and vegetables that are loaded with antioxidants, which help our skin to feel supple and nourished. If you find that getting your five a day is difficult, do what we do when you wake up bright-eyed and bushy-tailed in the morning. Make yourself a juice. You will have to invest in a juicer first, but they are worth the money. Then just feed the juicer any fruit and vegetables that you can find in your fridge. Try a delicious juice made with two celery sticks, one green pepper, half a cucumber and two apples. If it sounds revolting – try it! It is fresh, green and fabulous and will set you up for the day.

- Exercising on a regular basis increases the blood flow to the surface of our skin and helps to repair skin tissue, which in turn gives us a healthy glow.

- Invest in a good cleanser, toner, moisturiser and sunscreen.

- Keep your hair clean by washing it regularly. Try to avoid hair products and shampoos that are oily, as these products can transfer from hair to face, even at night time, which in turn can affect your skin. You should also change your pillow slip at least once a week to prevent oil from it affecting your skin.

- Try to stop touching your face. You are transferring bacteria from everything you have touched from your hands to your face. Furthermore, try to keep the receiver of your phone off your face; the dirt and germs that have built up on your phone can transfer to your skin.

- Check the labels on make-up and all skincare products. Don't use oil-based products. If using powder, be sure to wash the powder pad regularly.

- We are all aware of the importance of sunscreen for all skin types. Light lotion sunscreens will not irritate your skin and will help you to avoid the danger of skin cancer in later years.

- Do not squeeze or pick at spots. It only spreads bacteria and aggravates the tissue more.

- Try to use fragrance-free, unscented products to avoid skin sensitivities or allergies.

- Most mild cases of acne can be controlled at home by using these tips and using suitable products as part of a daily skincare routine. However, there are times when you need to go to the doctor or a dermatologist. Getting a facial from a specialist beautician can be helpful too.

- Be patient and stick with your skincare plan for a few weeks without getting discouraged.

I choose to focus on what I like about my face, rather than be upset about my spots. I am more than a reflection in a mirror.

Remember that there are two kinds of beauty: one of the soul and the other of the body.

Cervantes

PMS

Most girls experience discomfort just before and for the first few days of their period. However, for some, premenstrual syndrome (PMS) can be debilitating enough to interfere with school and daily activities and can even leave them bedridden and miserable. In addition to their monthly cycle, many girls have told us that they suffer from mood swings, irritability, anxiety, headaches, cramps, dizzy spells, bloating, fatigue and tender breasts. These symptoms can result from hormonal fluctuations in your cycle. Some of them are linked to prostaglandins that cause the uterine muscles to tighten, which results in cramping. A week to ten days before your period the hormone progesterone starts to drop, which can cause you to retain water and salt. This imbalance between oestrogen and progesterone contributes to symptoms such as irritability and anxiety.

Jokes about menstrual cramps are not funny. Period.

Anonymous

We asked students for **their** tips about what helped them when it came to the monthly agony of cramps and PMS – you may have to go through the list until you find one that works for you, but when you do, stick with it!

TIPS

✪ Heat helps to relax the contracting muscles in your uterus and the advice women have passed down through the generations is that a hot water bottle can literally be a girl's best friend for easing period pain.

✪ Although exercise is probably the furthest thing from your mind when you are curled up clutching a hot water bottle or heat pad to your stomach, it boosts the release of painkilling endorphins, which are feel-good chemicals that can also relax your muscles. Exercise combats fluid retention. If you are still not convinced, try some relaxing stretches or yoga postures in the comfort of your own living room!

✪ Massage your tummy to soothe the pain. You could use essential oil massage blends to relieve menstrual cramps. German chamomile is known for its ability to reduce inflammation. It is also good for calming irritability. Clary sage essential oil added to your bath is also effective for pain.

✪ Eat a well-balanced diet. Chocolate may put a smile on your face but it contains caffeine so it could make your cramps even worse. Try to avoid salt around this time as it affects water-retention levels, leading to more bloating, which you really don't want. Make an effort to eat more fruit, vegetables and wholegrains. High-fibre foods act as a natural laxative and help to remove excess oestrogen from your body.

✪ Drink lots of water. The more hydrated you are, the better. Natural diuretic foods such as celery, asparagus, garlic, parsley and watercress are good too.

✪ Chamomile and peppermint teas can relieve spasms by relaxing your uterus.

✪ Calcium is a muscle relaxant and can reduce PMS. If you are taking calcium supplements you should also take magnesium. Calcium can make you sleepy so take it late at night just before you go to bed.

✪ Magnesium deficiency is believed to be a leading cause of menstrual cramps. Students have found that supplementing with magnesium a few days before menstruation eased their symptoms. Alternatively, stock up on high-magnesium foods such as dark, leafy greens, avocados, wholegrains, nuts, seeds, fish, beans and bananas.

✪ Run yourself a bath and add a cup of Epsom salts, which are high in magnesium. (You can find these in your local health food shop.) A hot, soothing bath can help to relax the muscles of the body and the uterus and improve your sense of well-being. Alternatively, stand under a shower of warm water targeted towards your back or abdomen.

✪ B6 can combat irritability as it increases your supply of serotonin, which is a brain chemical. This vitamin is also known as the 'happy hormone', as it regulates mood swings. Good food sources of B6 include proteins such as fish, poultry and meat. It also reduces fatigue, sugar cravings, fluid retention and breast tenderness.

✪ Eating foods containing iron is essential for you, as they support growth. Iron can prevent anaemia, which can be caused by blood loss from heavy periods. Foods high in iron include wholegrains, red meat, chicken, turkey, eggs, lamb, dark leafy greens such as spinach, liver, sunflower seeds, beans, nuts and dark chocolate.

✪ Essential fatty acids (EFAs) are believed to slow down the production of prostaglandins which contribute to cramps. High essential fatty acids are found in fish, shellfish, leafy vegetables, pumpkin seeds, sunflower seeds and walnuts. A complete essential fatty acid supplement can also help you to get a wide variety of EFAs. Another effective supplement is B6 and evening primrose oil.

✪ Painkillers can be used to ease cramps but we think that it is worth trying natural remedies before resorting to taking medication. If you are taking medication always follow the directions on the label.

✪ If your periods are causing you significant pain, consult your doctor. He or she may need to prescribe an oral contraceptive, also known as the pill, which can lighten blood flow and address more extreme symptoms such as cramps, backache and vomiting.

✪ It is important to change your sanitary pad or tampon **throughout** the day and also to wash yourself even more regularly during this time. Have extra sanitary pads or tampons and clean underwear properly stored in a clean paper bag in your locker in school so you are prepared for anything!

Your Virtual World

Have you ever asked yourself why you spend so much of your precious time on Snapchat, Instagram and Facebook? Are you one of those people who believes that real life is what happens online? Do you break out in a cold sweat when you can't find your phone, because if the truth were told, you have a deep-seated fear of missing out (FOMO)? Do you check your posts constantly and a bit obsessively, comparing your status online with friends? Would the world really end tomorrow if you refused to check your phone for one day?

Social networking sites are not going away any time soon. A 2012 Common Sense Media study found that 78 per cent of teens have a profile on social media sites, 68 per cent text every day and 73 per cent use at least two types of these sites every day. Shockingly, 71 per cent of teenage girls say that they hide their online activity from their parents (Sass, 2012). So, before we all run for the hills, holding our heads in our hands in despair, we need to ask, 'How do we help teens to use the Internet wisely?'

Michelle Obama said, 'How on earth can we teach our girls to love and accept themselves in a world that is modelling the exact opposite behaviour, teaching them instead to seek approval and validation from everyone but themselves?' Girls, you need to go within and discover how strong, unique and wonderful you are. Why give your power away to people who will judge you online based solely on your appearance? You are more than two-bit soundbites on Facebook or Twitter – you are more than a snapshot on Instagram. For some girls, posting 'selfies' can turn into a competitive business. What starts out as a harmless bit of fun can quickly turn into an obsessive tallying of 'likes' and 'thumbs-up'. If your friend gets significantly more likes than you when she posts glamorous, sexy photos of herself online, how does that leave you feeling? Even if you are a veteran poster, social media can play havoc with your emerging sense of self-esteem.

You yourself, as much as anybody in the entire universe, deserve your love and affection.

Buddha

> Stop looking to the outside world for validation and your sense of self-worth. Learn to love yourself.

(S): A student of mine told me recently how difficult it is trying to navigate the world of social media. She recounted a story about her best friend who had put a photo of herself up on Facebook and had received two hundred 'likes'. This highly intelligent, attractive girl said that her fear was that she would not get a fraction of those likes if she were to do the same. Teens are growing up in an era where they must be popular not only among their own close-knit group of friends but also with their virtual friends. It is very hard to compete with all the distorted versions of reality that face young people every day when they turn on their smartphones or log on to their computers.

(M): In class, a student mentioned how frustrated she was recently when she was out with her friend on a bus going in to town. Her friend briefly introduced her to three other girls and then turned around and began talking to someone else entirely. This friend presumed that just because my student was friends with the three girls on Facebook that she would easily converse with them in real life. The opposite in fact was true. My student told me how she clammed up and felt extremely awkward. She quickly realised that being virtual friends with somebody is not quite the same thing as actually being real friends.

(M): It always makes me smile when students ask me with a look of utter amazement on their faces how I managed to conduct a social life without a mobile phone back in the prehistoric 1980s and 1990s. I tell them that it was not a problem, that, actually, if I am to be honest, life was (sorry!) much easier and less complicated back then. I didn't care what celebrities were wearing, what crazy diet they were enduring, I just wanted to have fun with my close friends. If we wanted to meet up, we would simply arrange a time and place to do so and turn up. When I say this, a lot of the time, the students laugh and look at me with pitying glances but I have noticed an increase in the amount of girls who say that they envy me and my carefree teenage years. Many of them wish deep down that they could switch off for a while. The Common Sense Media study tells us that 43 per cent of teenagers wish that they could unplug and 21 per cent wish that their parents would too.

Why is being online so addictive?

Look around you the next time you are out and about or sitting in a busy café enjoying a nice strong Americano. It seems like the whole world is talking or typing into their smartphones, oblivious to real life, which is going on all around them. Why is this? Why are our phones taking over our very existence and ruining social interaction? Have you ever been deep in conversation with someone when their phone rings and you are asked to wait while your friend takes the call or, worse, views a text or post? The message they are sending out is very clear – you are not as interesting as the person on the other end of the line.

Social media makes us feel a part of the world at large. If you post something intelligent and hilarious online and receive lots of likes for it, then chances are your feelings of self-worth will skyrocket, whether you want to admit this to yourself or not. Of course, remember that unfortunately the reverse of this is also true. In many ways online activities are a double-edged sword – they are both a positive and negative force to be reckoned with. If you think about it for a minute, you have the power to be a positive influence on the world, so why not tap into this power by posting kind and supportive messages about your friends, which will, in turn, help them to accept themselves for who they are on the inside and not how they look on the outside?

Social media and self-esteem

In school, we are forever telling the girls never to compare themselves to anyone else. We always remind them that they should learn to celebrate their individuality and not to be afraid of it. Social media, in many ways, does the exact opposite – it presents you with versions of reality that have been airbrushed, distorted and cropped to within an inch of their lives. Often what is being presented to you is merely an illusion. In today's technological world, you are comparing yourself to not only your own classmates but images of people from all over the world. Unfortunately, we live in a world which celebrates youth, beauty and being impossibly slender. Look at any reality TV programme, read any magazine telling us how we can lose ten pounds in two weeks and watch any advertisement on TV promoting beauty products which promise to eliminate wrinkles, spots or blemishes in the wink of an eye. You don't have to be Einstein to realise that our modern world places a huge emphasis on physical perfection, whatever that means.

Recently, a group of senior students answered two questions put to them about social media. The first one was how long they spent daily on social media sites and the second was whether or not they regarded social media as a friend or a foe. Their responses were interesting. The amount of time spent online varied from forty minutes to four hours (which is rather worrying). What surprised us more was the fact that many of them regarded social media as a foe rather than a friend. Others said that, if used correctly, **it was a good thing** and the rest said that they simply couldn't live without it! There is no doubt that teenagers today spend more time in front of a screen than ever before. However, remember that while your screens educate and entertain you, they are also shaping your perceptions of yourself, whether you like it or not.

Using the Internet safely

Know the importance of face-to-face, real friendships. It is good to talk. And remember that nothing is private on the net. In 2014 a forensic psychologist came in to talk to the juniors in our school about their Internet use. She asked how many of them had more than a hundred friends on Facebook and the entire hall raised their hands. Then she asked how many had more than five hundred friends online and a staggering amount of girls (most of them under fifteen) put up their hands. She then proceeded to question whether they would walk down a busy shopping street in any town in Ireland and hand a folder with all their personal information inside to the first stranger that they met. Of course, everyone said that they would never do such a thing. The speaker informed the group that that is **exactly** what they are doing when they befriend total strangers online.

Everything you put online is permanent. Once you post a photo it is no longer owned by you. It is owned by Instagram or Facebook, or whatever site you have posted on. Texts, pictures and posts can go viral within hours. Posting inappropriate material could also have serious implications down the line. When you apply to a university or for a job you will most likely be researched online. If you post things online that you later regret, that content may never disappear, so stop to think before you post. Deleted does not mean gone. It just means you have to look a little harder for it.

Remember this before you post anything online:

T	=	Is it true?
H	=	Is it helpful?
I	=	Is it inspiring?
N	=	Is it necessary?
K	=	Is it kind?

It's OK to keep some parts of your life,
and your self, private.

False truths

Don't believe everything you read or see on people's profiles. Many exaggerate how wonderful their lives are to impress and perhaps to make online friends jealous. Some use apps such as Perfect365, which banishes blemishes, erases under-eye dark circles, brightens skin, whitens teeth and enhances eyelashes, in order to touch up their photos before they post them on social media. The app promises to be your 'one-stop-shop for magazine-worthy digital makeovers'. While all this sounds marvellous, the subtext is rather disturbing – the underlying message here is that you simply are not pretty enough just as you are. Therefore, in order to present yourself to go online, you must first fabricate a better, more streamlined, brighter than bright (but essentially artificial) version of yourself because your real self won't do. How crazy is this?

Others such as Whisper let users share their deepest, darkest secrets anonymously with millions of others in cyberspace. On its appstore listing, the site proudly states, 'with Whisper you're fine to anonymously share your thoughts with the world!' However, the danger is that vicious rumours get posted. With Snapchat you are led to believe that once you send a photo it will disappear 'forever' after thirty seconds. However, the truth is that it is very easy to screen-shot this image, so don't post anything that you would not let your parents see.

Realise that social media is an important part of your life but it is not actually real life. Many students say that they feel anxious and irritable when they don't have their phones nearby. Why? Stop and think about the power this small device has over you. Why do you hate the thought of missing out on what's happening online? Is it because you **feel that real life is what happens online?**

Make your 'offline life' – your real life – your priority.

Sexting

Sexting occurs when you send other people sexual pictures of yourself or people you know. Please remember, girls – never allow anyone to take or receive a highly sexualised photo of you. Ask yourself, 'Why do they want this photo in the first place?'

These pictures can be shared. Think about what your parents, neighbours, teachers and friends would say if they saw it. You need to bear in mind that it is against the law to be in possession of a sexually explicit photo of someone who is under the age of seventeen and if you post such images online you could be charged with the distribution of child pornography. Lastly, think about your future before you post anything and ask yourself if your online behaviour could jeopardise your future career prospects. If the answer is yes, don't do it.

Selfies – self-expression or self-absorption?

The Poetics of the Selfie

The *Oxford English Dictionary* named 'selfie' Word of the Year last year and defines it as a 'photograph that one has taken of oneself, typically when taken with a smartphone and uploaded to a social media website'.

What are the benefits of posting selfies online? Many teens say that it enhances their social status. However, as mentioned earlier, there is a flip-side. Posting photos of yourself online means that you are exposing yourself to all sorts of comments and criticism from people you don't even know.

We have all heard of Ask FM and similar sites which can damage young lives forever. The very things that you yearn for, i.e. validation and approval, are being sought in cyberspace, which by its very nature is anonymous. So many of you are having your confidence crushed by negative online comments. Remember, what other people think of you is not only completely out of your control, but also not really important in the first place. It is an entirely pointless exercise worrying about what the world and cyberspace think about you. Why would you want to hand over control to people you barely know?

Why not join a homework club where you can actually make a real difference to some young child's life? Maybe you could visit a local old folks' home and offer to help out? Perhaps you could contact a local animal rescue centre and offer your time? If you are sporty, what about offering to train a local under-10s team? The point here is that instead of becoming obsessed with what virtual people are doing (or not doing), you could actually be helping the community at large. Not only that, but you will find yourself energised by helping someone who really needs it. As a result, self-esteem will develop. Instead of focusing inwards, maybe it's time to turn our gaze outwards to the real world.

'If we could take selfies of our souls, would they be attractive enough to post?

Anonymous

Log out, walk tall and get out into the real world!

Door Out of the Dark

Some years ago, a student was asked to speak in front of the class. The student in question was bright, bubbly and popular. The exercise was to tell her classmates about her likes and dislikes. She proceeded to do so and told us a little bit about her world and how she saw herself in it. At the end of her speech, she revealed that she suffers with depression and how, despite appearances, she feels low a lot of the time. This was an incredibly brave thing for her to do. She was fifteen.

A 2013 article in the *Irish Independent* stated that 'the World Health Organisation (WHO) predicts that by 2030, depression will be the number one global health problem'. 'Globally, the organisation says that 20pc of children and teenagers will experience a disabling mental health problem. And doctors agree that the most common age of onset of major depression is around 13 or 14.'

When I feel down or troubled I sometimes wonder if I am actually depressed or if I'm just going through a rough stage and simply in a prolonged bad mood?

For some, adolescence can be a nightmare. Gone are the days of childhood innocence and fun and in their place is a time which can be fraught with stresses and anxieties. It is very understandable to feel sad, confused and lonely from time to time. If we think in stereotypes, teens are often presented as being anti-social, moody and disengaged. This is normal, right? To some extent, yes, absolutely. However, a problem arises when the negative thoughts and feelings do not go away …

When you are depressed you can feel like the loneliest person in the world. It is as if you are the only one feeling like this and, often, teens are slow to speak about exactly how they feel for fear of being further isolated. Unfortunately, there is still a stigma attached to mental illness in Ireland, although this is slowly changing. People are terrified of appearing weak or somehow flawed to the world at large. Students who are depressed in school often say that they fear being judged more than anything. They are terrified that people will tell them to 'snap out of it' or that it is just a phase they are going through when it is not. They fear that the way they feel will last forever and they often think that they will have to exist like this indefinitely. As a result many will initially try to deal with their depression alone, which only serves to worsen the problem.

(M): A few years ago I listened to a young man talking eloquently about his depression. He said that living with this condition is like living in a black and white world because depression drains all the colour out of life.

Depression is far more common than you think. What is important is that you reach out to someone you love and tell them **exactly** how you feel. Do not sugar-coat how you are feeling to protect a loved one: tell them everything. Girls are much quicker to tell you when something is wrong than boys. Unfortunately, a lot of the time (although not always), boys still find it harder to admit that there is a problem.

If you are feeling depressed, it can be very hard to do anything about it. You may find it difficult simply getting out of bed in the morning and dragging yourself into school. This is why it is so important to tell friends or family. You need to let others take over if you feel that you cannot cope. Friends are wonderful: they know when something is wrong and are often the first to pick up on the clues that something is amiss. If you suspect that a close friend is feeling depressed, do something about it today. Tell them that you are worried about them, that you are there for them and ask them honestly what you can do for them. If they push you away and deny that anything is wrong when clearly it is, then you need to enlist the help of a supportive adult. **Do not try to deal with this alone.** And remember there is always hope. Even if your depression is chronic and is absolutely crippling you, there is always a silver lining.

(S): Everyone thought one particular student I taught 'had it all', she was gorgeous, clever, funny and popular or so it seemed. Internally the pain she suffered day and night was unbearable.

She felt like she was drowning in a sea of self-loathing. She kept thinking that she could battle her inner demons and that her overwhelming feelings of depression would disappear. However, the dark shadows seemed to follow her everywhere. She felt imprisoned and shut out even when surrounded by others. She felt like she didn't belong. She was so terribly alone. Eventually, she realised that she couldn't win this particular battle alone. When she reached out and asked for help life became easier. Almost immediately she began to realise her life really was worth fighting for, so fight she did.

Examining negative thoughts

Depression can make you lose sight of the person you once were. It can be beyond difficult to think about and perceive things clearly when you are feeling depressed. It is not simply a case of pulling yourself together. However, the way you are thinking could be adding to your problems.

✦ *Are you impossibly hard on yourself? Do you always expect more from yourself than you are able to give? Do you have to be the best at everything you do?* Maybe it is time to ditch this perfectionism. If you think that you are a perfectionist, you might need to examine why it is that you put so much pressure on yourself.

✦ *Drop the word 'should' from your vocabulary.* Stop telling yourself things you should be doing. Instead ask yourself, 'Why should I?'

✦ *Are you an all-or-nothing type of person? Do you look at the world in black and white?* Remember, life is not only about black and white: there is plenty of grey also. Do you say to yourself, 'If I don't get an A-grade in my Maths test then I am a complete and utter failure'?

✦ *Do you jump to conclusions without having any concrete evidence to* hand? Do you say things to yourself like 'I really like John but he is obviously not interested in me because he never even looked my way tonight'? For all you know, John could have a million and one things on his mind, he could have received bad news and it is possible that he didn't even see you.

✦ *Do you believe that because you **feel** terrible you **are** terrible?* The way you feel does not define you. When depression strikes, it can be hard to recognise yourself. However, never tell yourself that you are a failure because you feel the way you do.

✦ *Do you find that you ignore positive things in your life and instead you zone in on the negative?* I think all of us are guilty of doing this from time to time. If you get an assignment back in school, do you only focus on the more critical comments the teacher may have written and ignore all the positive feedback and praise they gave you?

✦ *Do you generalise all of the time?* If you make one mistake, do you tell yourself that you never get **anything** right? How accurate or helpful is this?

What can I do to get better?

Be realistic. Baby steps are needed when starting off on the road to recovery. The problem with depression is that it saps you of all energy and vitality so that it is hard to make a movement in the right direction. We all know that exercise is an effective tool in combating depression, but how do you muster up the energy to go for a five-mile run when taking a shower is more than you can manage? I suppose we need to realise that **there is a difference between something that is difficult and something that is impossible**. One of the problems with depression is that the very things that can help you to feel better are often too hard to contemplate, let alone carry out. So, forget the five-mile run, but ask yourself if you could manage the shower. Better still, talk to somebody today, even if it is only for five minutes.

Give yourself lots of time; take things very gently indeed. Try to remember that all you have to deal with is this moment: don't tell yourself that this is the way you will feel for the rest of your life, as that is simply not true. When feeling depressed, days can seem to last forever: just concentrate on right here, right now.

Take one minute at a time, one day at a time.

TIPS TO HELP YOU COPE

'Finish each day and be done with it.
You have done what you could ...
Tomorrow is a new day.'
Ralph Waldo Emerson

✪ **Enlist the help of your close friends and family.** They are the people who love you most in the world, they want to help you to get better but they cannot if you refuse to let them in. Having friends around, even if you do not feel like it, will ensure that you feel less isolated and this is important in the recovery process. Even if you feel (and you probably do) that nobody understands you, keep your friends close at hand. They will offer you a different perspective. If you need your friends to listen to you or simply sit quietly in the same room while you all watch a movie, tell them. Make them feel less anxious about the situation – explain that you do not expect them to be magicians; you know that they cannot cure you, but having them around helps. That is enough.

✪ **Get the professional help you need.** Visit your GP today if you feel that your depression is too much to deal with. They can listen to you and recommend steps to take to ensure your recovery. They can also put you in touch with counsellors who can help you to understand your illness and enable you to get better.

❂ **What about finding out if there are any support groups in your area?** Often, talking to like-minded people can really help when you feel lost and alone. Listening to other people's stories may offer you some insights into your situation. A support group will make you see that there are many other people out there struggling with life (for whatever reasons) just like you. There is often comfort in knowing this.

'What you are is what you have been, and what you will be is what you do now.'

Buddha

❂ **If possible, arrange to go out with friends once a week.** This does not have to be anything too daunting – you could simply arrange to meet one of your best friends for a coffee. If you don't feel like talking, go to a movie. The important thing is that you are getting up, getting dressed and getting out of the house and into the outside world, even if it is only for a short while.

❂ **Look after yourself.** We mention this in the chapter on anxiety. It is so important to take care of yourself when feeling depressed. So what can you do to help and aid recovery? Are you taking any of the steps in this list?

❂ **Try to eat three healthy, nutritious meals every day.** Many people, when they are stressed or depressed, lose their appetite – they stop deriving pleasure from eating delicious, healthy foods. Think of food as medicine – try to eat as much fresh, local and nutritious food as possible. Cut down on or even eliminate junk food and refined (white) carbohydrates. Opt instead for wholewheat bread, pasta and rice: they release energy slowly and keep you fuller for longer. Take B vitamins: they can help with mood swings and tiredness. Avoid alcohol at all costs: it will only make you feel worse. Get your fill of super foods such as spinach, avocados, brown rice, bananas, quinoa and butternut squash. Not only are these foods good to eat, but they are good for mind and body also.

✪ **Try to get a decent amount of sleep every night.** Again, students often tell us that sleep is the first thing to be affected when they are feeling depressed. Keep a routine – go to bed and get up at the same time every day. Whatever you do, avoid the temptation to stay in bed sleeping all day; you will just find that you are up half the night. Being the only one awake while the entire house is sleeping soundly will do nothing to help feelings of isolation. Do not let tiredness become a part of how you see yourself.

✪ **Get out into the fresh air every day.** We all need our daily dose of sunlight and people with depression need it even more. So, grab the dog and go for a short walk, even if you really don't want to. Likewise, in school do not stop participating in sport, especially if you enjoyed it in the past. If you can at all, keep it up. Not only will the exercise improve your mood (it is now widely regarded as the best natural antidepressant there is), but you will be meeting and interacting with other school friends. Try to continue some of the things you enjoyed before depression struck. Do not let depression rob you of your old life. **You are still you: that has not changed, even if the way you feel has.** Don't lose sight of who you are – you are more than depression. Don't forget that.

✪ **Practise mindfulness, yoga or any relaxation technique that appeals to you.** It has now been scientifically proven that regular practising of mindfulness can significantly help to reduce symptoms of stress, anxiety and depression. Find out whatever you can about classes in your area and bring a parent or friend along with you if you don't fancy going alone.

Please don't suffer in silence.

Even though you may think that your life is out of control and you are spiralling deeper and deeper towards the abyss, don't be ashamed of or afraid of your feelings. Reach out to someone today if you are worried that depression is an issue for you. Take one day at a time and look after yourself. Tell yourself over and over that you can overcome depression, even though this may seem like an exhausting and extremely difficult thing to do. You can get your life back and never forget that there is always a reason to face tomorrow. Take care.

When It Feels Like It's Too Much ...

Is your self-esteem at an all-time low? Do your thoughts sometimes frighten or disturb you? Is it hard for you to go on? There are times when no matter what we do or how hard we try, life overwhelms us and we just don't know what path to follow or who to confide in. Sometimes the most courageous thing to do is to let go, surrender and admit to yourself and somebody you love that you need help, because you don't want to go on living this way.

★ ★ ★

Your feelings of self-loathing and despair do not mean that you are somehow flawed or a failure. Underneath all of the pain, hurt, confusion and fear you are still you, even if you find it hard some days to recognise yourself. Everybody hurts. If your distress is too much to bear, reach out and seek medical help.

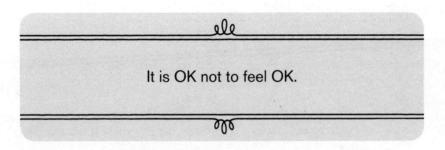

It is OK not to feel OK.

Eating disorders

Eating disorders are extremes in eating behaviour. They are linked to a person's self-worth and always require expert medical care. The exact causes of such disorders remain unknown, but psychological, environmental and social factors are thought to be contributing factors. There are many theories but no definitive answers. The most common disorders are Bulimia Nervosa and Anorexia Nervosa. Other food-related disorders, like body-image disorders, binging and food phobias are becoming more prevalent. According to the Irish Health Research Board in 2013, females accounted for 92 per cent of all admissions of those affected by eating disorders. Many develop eating disorders between the ages of thirteen and seventeen. These disorders are not just a problem for girls – boys and men suffer too.

Eating disorders can develop quickly and are very serious. Watch out for them in friends. Wrought with insecurities, teens often look to the media for instruction on how to look, what to wear, how to act and even what to think. Being healthy and exercising are important to all of us. However, sometimes extreme behaviours in eating habits can lead to people becoming seriously ill and can have life-threatening consequences.

> Ask for help and take the first step towards a better and brighter tomorrow.

Could I have an eating disorder?

✦ Do you ever feel like thoughts about weight and food are controlling your life?

✦ Or that after eating certain foods you deserve to be punished by not allowing yourself to eat later on or by exercising in excess to compensate for eating it?

✦ Are parents' requests for you to eat properly and exercise moderately irritating you, as you worry that they are sabotaging your weight-loss plan?

If you have answered yes to these questions, it may be time to find the inner strength to admit that you might have an eating disorder. It can be scary to admit it to yourself, or to ask for help, but do not let fear stop you from getting the help you need. Admitting that you might have a problem and talking to someone about it are major steps forward.

TIPS FOR SEEKING HELP

✪ An understanding doctor who will validate your experience is your first port of call. He/she can advise you about how to get vital nutrients back into your diet and how to fuel your body properly.

✪ A therapist who has experience of working with eating disorders can make an incredibly positive difference if you can manage to be honest and brave enough to inform them of your thoughts, fears and behaviours.

✪ Research support groups in your area where you can hear testimonials from others in recovery. By doing this, you may feel less alone and become inspired by what others have gone through. Recovery is different for everyone, so what worked for your friend may not work for you. Be willing to try whatever it takes to get better.

✪ Your family and friends want to help, so don't shut them out. Be honest with them: this will help you to feel less alone. Let them support you during and after your recovery.

✪ Be nice to yourself. Forgive yourself if you relapse. With the help of your family and medical professionals, have a plan in place to deal with the setbacks.

✪ Feelings of depression and hopelessness can make it feel like what you are going through will last forever, but with determination, hard work, self-belief and support you can have a normal life again.

✪ In some cases medication is necessary to deal with health consequences linked with eating disorders.

Reach out today with confidence. You can get better!

You deserve to get help.

Self-harm

'Although the world is full of suffering,
it is also full of the overcoming of it.'

Helen Keller

This is also largely an issue which affects teenage girls. However, Rachel Welch, who is the project director of the website selfharm.co.uk, warns us that society should not assume boys do not self-harm, saying that 'because of the way society has constructed the image of self-harm, it makes it much easier for girls to come forward and ask for help'.

People who self-harm usually do not want to die – they are just trying to cope with the pain they are feeling inside. However, frequent self-harm needs to be taken seriously as there is a greater risk of suicide, which is why it's so important to look for help.

Thankfully, self-harm does not crop up very often in school, but when it does it is very distressing for all involved.

(M): A few years ago, a student was self-harming. The girl in question was bright, confident and great fun to be around. But underneath her cheerful exterior, she harboured deep-seated feelings of insecurity and self-loathing. For her, harming herself was a way to release feelings of frustration, rage and despair. It finally emerged that she had a very distorted self-image: she never felt pretty enough or clever enough when she compared herself to her peers, despite lots of evidence to the contrary. She felt that she was always competing with herself and again and again she felt that she fell short of who she wanted to be.

Lots of people find this whole idea difficult to grasp. Some people viewed the student in question as a 'drama queen'. In their eyes, her self-harming was an attempt to get attention. This couldn't have been further from the truth. Most teenagers who self-harm do so in private. Sometimes it can seem like the only thing that offers relief from feelings of intense sadness and pain. This student confessed that she actually felt better when she drew blood; it was a case of the physical pain obliterating the emotional upheaval. She said that harming herself gave her a sense of control and she admitted that she felt less anxious after an episode of self-harming. She felt this was her way of expressing and dealing with her distress. The only way she knew how to deal with her emotional pain was to injure herself. It sounds counterintuitive but she felt hurting herself made her feel better. However, this relief is only short-lived and sooner or later the old feelings of disgust and repulsion may rise to the surface again.

'Your skin is not paper, don't cut it. Your size isn't a book, don't judge it. Your life isn't a film, don't end it. Your story is an inspiration, be proud of it.'

⚡ Anonymous ⚡

How can I help a friend who may be self-harming?

The important thing is to accept her exactly how she is now. Tell her that you love her no matter what is playing out in her life at the moment. Try not to judge her or change her in any way, but instead ask her what she needs from you to help her to get better. It is vital that you don't pressurise her into talking about issues that she is unable or unwilling to talk about. Do not ask to see her scars. Never tell her that she is over-reacting. Instead, reassure her that whatever is going on with her right now is OK. Explain that she will get better and that you are going to help her every step of the way. Encourage her to ask for help and remind her that she does not have to go through this alone, that you are there for her. Always try to persuade her to ask for help even if the thought of doing so terrifies her.

Suicide

About two years ago, there seemed to be a spate of teen suicides in our area. On one particular occasion a young man took his own life. When this happens, it affects the entire community. Although the boy who died so tragically did not go to our school, his untimely death had a ripple effect in that the sadness which resulted from it spread outwards. Everyone was devastated and hardly knew what to do with themselves. Some of the girls who knew him well said that they felt guilty that they were still alive and he was not. Our school principal talked to them, reminding them how suicide was a long-term solution to a short-term problem. How can these young people bear such tragedy – especially as it seems to be occurring regularly in towns up and down our country? Nothing is ever quite the same after a good friend dies in this way and the group of friends may suffer collectively or individually.

If a close friend tells you that they are feeling suicidal, they mean it. Perhaps they are tired of feeling the way they do and, to them, suicide is a way of getting rid of the pain which consumes them and refuses to go away. It is important that they receive support and understanding at this difficult time. If your friend has reached crisis point, get help now. Tell them that you will always be there for them but do not try to deal with your friend's behaviour alone – it is simply too much to take on.

Time and time again the students mention Donal Walsh's name in class. To them, this young man was, and is, a legend. In his short life, he managed to impress an entire nation. For those of you who do not know, Donal lost his battle to cancer in 2013 but before he left us he spoke to teenagers about suicide. This is what he said:

I realised that I was fighting for my life for the third time in four years and this time I have no hope. Yet still I hear of young people committing suicide. For these people, no matter how bad life gets, there are no reasons bad enough to make them do this … So please, as a 16-year-old who has no say in his death sentence, who has no choice in the pain he is about to cause and who would take any chance at even a few more months on this planet, appreciate what you have, know that there are other options and help is always there.

If you feel like you cannot go on, tell someone. Sometimes, taking the first step is the hardest. Things will get better. You have to hang on to that belief. If you cannot help yourself, then let somebody else look after you for a while.

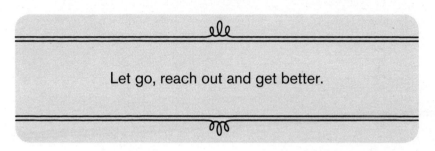

Let go, reach out and get better.

Under Pressure

For Olympic athletes a heightened state of alert can be useful when it comes to performing well – the same is true during your final exams. A word of warning, though: being under constant academic pressure is not beneficial to anybody. Ask yourself is it time to calm down and take control of the situation?

Studying consists of learning a set of skills and, like anything, must be practised in order for you to peak. By developing study skills, stress management techniques, coping strategies and understanding learning styles, you can help to alleviate pressure and succeed where before you might have struggled.

Getting started is always difficult – however, once you are in a routine, things will get easier. Think for a moment about somebody preparing for, say, the Dublin marathon. They never start off at a flat-out sprint. The same applies to your study. Pace yourself, and find a level of speed and stamina which is right for you and which you can maintain. Concentrate on small, attainable goals rather than trying to scale the entire mountain. Make one little change to start with. Every time you succeed, congratulate yourself and continue to raise the bar a little higher. Once you have reached a certain point, it can be easy to relax these habits. If you slip up do not indulge in catastrophic thinking patterns. Instead, focus on the long-term goal. Pick yourself up and keep moving forward. Challenge yourself and you will be pleasantly surprised to see where you are this time next year.

'Always bear in mind that your own resolution to succeed is more important than any one thing.'

Abraham Lincoln

Intelligence vs academic achievement

It can be frustrating when you are working hard and yet your efforts do not merit the grade that you had envisioned. Do not let grades undermine your sense of self-worth or stop you striving for your goals. All you can do is your best. The biggest misconception about intelligence and academic achievement is that they are equivalent to each other. We all learn differently.

During the school year, students can become preoccupied to the point of distraction with the idea that academic results and grades represent who they are. We are all unique, we all have different strengths. Like the old saying goes: it is not how intelligent you are, but how you are intelligent.

Students with learning difficulties say that academic pressure can affect their self-esteem. They often have a sense of inferiority when compared to their peers and this throws up roadblocks ahead of their own chances of success. Discovering that something may stand in the way of your success can be unsettling. However, it is important for you to understand that it does not mean that you are less intelligent than anyone else: you just learn differently. Your brain receives, processes and communicates information in a way that is less typical. If you have a learning difficulty you may have trouble processing sensory information because you see, hear and understand the world differently.

'Everybody is a genius. But if you judge a fish by its ability to climb a tree, it will live its whole life believing that it is stupid.'

Unknown

Common sense vs academic intelligence

Grades measure your performance in school, but your performance in life in general is measured by intelligence. The challenge at school is to retain as much knowledge as possible. In life the challenge is to make intelligent decisions and progress. Life has a different plan for each of us. Just because academia may not be your forte does not mean that you are destined to fail. This perhaps is the difference between your intelligence and knowledge, compared to your wisdom and worldliness. You too will find your area of strength and shine.

Intelligence does not necessarily predicate success in life. To this day, the jury is still out when it comes to how we define intelligence. In 1983 Dr Howard Gardner, a psychologist and professor of neuroscience from Harvard University, developed the theory of Multiple Intelligences. According to Gardner, there is more to genius than a high IQ. Cognitive tests measure IQ, cognitive ability, intelligence and mental ability. Gardner argues that there is no one true way to measure intelligence, as IQ tests cannot take into account the vast array of different talents which people have. He believes that the human brain is wired with a wide range of cognitive abilities. We have all heard of musical geniuses who struggle with comprehension or amazing linguists who cannot fathom algebra or the mathematician who is weak on emotional and social intelligence.

If we could all start to celebrate our abilities as components of intelligence, the world would be a smarter and more accepting place.

Focusing

Do you ever find yourself wasting time before you actually knuckle down to your homework? Does the prospect of cleaning the entire house from top to bottom seem like a much more enjoyable alternative to actually beginning your *Othello* essay due in last week?

Do you fool yourself regularly, telling yourself that you are super-productive when the reality is that you spend most of your study time staring out the window, asleep on your bed or checking your smartphone for all the latest gossip?

If all this sounds familiar, be brutally honest with yourself. Identify distractions such as Snapchat or Facebook and remove them from your study zone. Do it today. The best way to beat procrastination is to get started!

Below are some techniques which we have found effective to help clear the mind and focus. Remember, different strategies work for different people, so experiment with the various techniques to see which ones work best for you. By doing this, you are taking responsibility for your own well-being.

Techniques to help you focus

✦ Thought-stopping can help you to let go of negative thoughts and change them to ones that can help you to feel calmer and more relaxed. The basis of this technique is that you consciously tell yourself to 'Stop!' when you experience recurrent negative or frightening thoughts. You then replace the negative thought with something more positive, manageable and realistic. Instead of telling yourself 'I'm never going to be able to study enough for this test; I have such a bad memory', change it to the more positive statement 'I know I have a lot to learn but if I use the study skills that suit my learning style and stick to my schedule, I know I can do it.'

✦ Affirmations are short, powerful, positive statements about something that we would like to reinforce in our conscious mind. How many times have you told yourself 'I've got so much homework to do; I'll never get it all done'? Why not change this to the more positive phrase 'I can get all my homework done; I'm just going to have to use my time wisely and stop watching so much TV.' When you do this you will reduce your stress levels, which in turn will help you to finish your homework. Other examples include:

- 'I realise that this is the perfect time for me to study and prepare for the future and I am doing this.'
- 'I understand that habits make a person and right now I am developing good study habits.'
- 'I can overcome this obstacle.'

✦ Visualise a scene that makes you feel totally calm – imagine yourself at the beach, relaxing, watching the beautiful blue sky and the waves lapping against the shore. Every time you start to get stressed, picture your ideal place until you are relaxed and focused again.

✦ Learning to manage time makes it much easier to stay calm. Use a diary to schedule and record commitments. Leave yourself reminder notes if you are forgetful. Planning ahead is vital. Do not leave things to the last minute! When you are preparing a study plan or timetable, make sure that it leaves sufficient time for fun and relaxation, which are important components in any teen's life. Plan your revision and make sure that you set achievable targets. Watch your confidence grow as you meet your goals. Practise doing exam questions. If the question is expected to be completed in thirty minutes in the exam, see if you can answer it at home in the same amount of time. This can be really challenging at first but the more you do it, the faster and more focused you will become.

✦ On the day of the test, arrive in plenty of time so you are not flustered. Even though obsessive clock-watching is not to be recommended, do pay attention to the allotted time given for each question. Focus on yourself; do not keep checking the progress of other students during the test.

In life, most things take time and practice and learning to overcome exam anxiety is the very same. Dealing with exam pressure will help you to learn stress management, which is a valuable life skill. Different techniques work for different people, so find the right technique for you. It might take time, but keep practising.

Keep calm and stay strong. You can do this!

Study skills

By taking control of your study schedule, you can significantly reduce exam stress. Even the most confident student can be affected by nerves. We all know that some stress can be beneficial when it comes to motivating you to study, but it becomes a problem if you are so anxious that you are unable to focus and learn.

When you are feeling overwhelmed with your workload it can be difficult to produce high-quality work. Studying hard and not getting the grades you deserve is frustrating in the extreme. If you are putting in the work and the hours and it is simply not showing in your results, it might be time to try some new strategies and figure out what style of learning allows you to remember information efficiently. It is our behaviour more than our learned intelligence that will determine our success in life.

We are all unique. There is no universal method which works for everyone. Many students feel that they are just going through the motions and they are unable to retain information properly. Whether you are reading, studying or drawing diagrams, it is vital that the information is being stored in your memory. Practising different types of activities will give you a better understanding of your subjects and should help to improve concentration levels and information retention because you will have a greater interest in what you are doing.

It can be a struggle for students when they are trying to study in ways that are not natural for them. Utilising a variety of techniques can help you to succeed in school to the best of your ability. Students are usually divided into four categories: the visual learner, the auditory learner, the kinaesthetic learner and the read/write learner. Not every strategy will be effective for you. It is a case of trial and error when it comes to figuring out what helps to make studying easier.

Characteristics of the visual learner

✳ They learn best through what they see.

✳ The visual learner often creates strong pictures in their mind when they are reading.

✳ They benefit from illustrations, diagrams and visual presentations.

✳ They often close their eyes to visualise and remember.

✳ Bright colours appeal to them.

✳ They are good at reading maps and charts.

✳ Language, spoken or written, rich in pictorial imagery appeals to them; they have good imaginations.

✳ They tend to take lots of notes.

✳ They tend to be good readers.

Study tips best suited to the visual learner

✳ Use diagrams and charts while you study and ensure they are labelled properly.

✳ There are many free educational videos available online and they are a fantastic resource for studying at home.

✳ Use mind maps (explained below) whenever you can. The two main aspects of your memory – imagination and association – are used when you make mind maps. Some students prefer to use the online mind-mapping programmes.

✳ Highlight material in different colours so that you can visualise the information and remember it in terms of blocks of colour.

✳ Flashcards, which are often associated with the kinaesthetic learner, are also very useful for the visual learner, if diagrams are used on the cards.

✳ When you are trying to remember information, you should close your eyes and visualise it.

✳ When you are learning a new word, you should visualise the spelling of the word. When taking notes, replace words with symbols wherever possible.

✳ If you are typing up notes, you should use different fonts in order to make the most important concepts and facts visually apparent.

Characteristics of the auditory learner

✳ Auditory learners learn best when information is presented through the spoken word.

✳ Auditory learners tend to have an impressive memory for music, lyrics, jokes and conversations.

✳ They tend to prefer presenting information in an oral format instead of a written report. They enjoy debates and discussions.

✳ Interpreting complicated graphs or diagrams can pose a problem.

✳ This type of learner remembers best by verbalising and they often like to read aloud. They much prefer to take in information by discussing a topic or through audio or video clips.

✳ They do not tend to take a lot of notes in class as they are able to ingest what they need simply by paying attention and listening carefully.

Study tips best suited to the auditory learner

✳ Listening to audio recordings or audio books that relate to the topic you are studying can be very beneficial.

✳ Make up rhymes, mnemonics, jingles and songs to help remember information.

✳ Using features on devices that can read back the information to you or downloading the book so you can listen to the information as frequently as you need it can be very successful.

✳ Close your eyes and repeat information, facts and definitions out loud to yourself, or paraphrase the main points of what you have learned and then say it aloud.

✳ Use voice dictations to speak to your technology – the words you speak will appear typed.

✳ Sit at the front of the class in order to reduce distractions so you can hear what the teacher is saying.

✳ When you are proofreading you should read aloud. Also, solving maths problems out loud can be helpful.

✳ Auditory learners should ask questions in class because when ideas are put into words they can understand them much better.

✳ Watching DVDs and YouTube clips can be beneficial for the auditory learner as well as the visual learner.

✳ Teaching your parents or anyone who is willing to listen is also a very effective and hugely successful strategy for the auditory learner.

✳ Listening to music can be unhelpful for the auditory learner as they tend to get distracted by the lyrics.

Characteristics of the kinaesthetic learner

✳ The kinaesthetic/tactile learner has a 'hands-on brain'. They learn best doing, designing, experimenting, role playing, building and being involved. They are often good with their hands.

* When a kinaesthetic learner is bored they tend to fidget. They can find it difficult to sit still for long periods of time.

* The kinaesthetic learner needs to take frequent breaks and has a desire to move around and be active.

* Manipulating materials in practical subjects is very enjoyable, as they often rely on what they can directly experience. These students often enjoy Home Economics, Technology and PE.

* The kinaesthetic learner often speaks with their hands and by means of gestures.

* The kinaesthetic learner often enjoys books that are adventure based.

* The kinaesthetic learner is good at remembering things they have done before, like assembling things, making puzzles and cooking meals.

Study tips best suited to the kinaesthetic learner

* Movement is very beneficial to the kinaesthetic learner. When you are studying you should try to be physically active. Instead of just sitting at your desk, try pacing back and forth with your book or notes and read the information out loud.

* Typing keeps your mind active. Use the computer and the Internet to help you as you study.

* In order to keep yourself from getting distracted in class, try taking extensive written notes. Later, at home, you can edit and type them.

* Squeezing a stress ball or using a fidget toy can help, as it allows you to stay physically active while studying. However, if it becomes a distraction in itself, don't use it.

* Moving a coloured ruler along the page as you read keeps you active and focused.

* Act out or make models of things you have to learn whenever you can.

* Even though you need to study as much as everyone else, short blocks of study with frequent small breaks work best for you. Walk around during your break.

✻ Some kinaesthetic learners find it hard to focus sitting upright at a desk, so lying on their back or tummy can be helpful for them.

✻ Flashcards work very well when you write questions on one side and answers on the other – they can become an active game to play on your own or with someone.

✻ When you are trying to retain information, try closing your eyes and imagine that you are writing the information in the air. Picture the information in your mind as you do it. Some people like to use a dry-erase or chalk-board to study or review.

✻ Using concrete objects to understand maths and other concepts can be helpful. Younger learners find using letter blocks to remember spellings very useful.

✻ Use different-coloured highlighters when reviewing and studying.

Characteristics of the read/write learner

✻ They are avid readers and copious note-takers so they often fit in with the conventional method of writing notes and reading textbooks.

✻ A read/write learner often finds that they study best by reading over their notes or copying them out.

✻ They prefer working in a quiet environment on their own to avoid distractions.

✻ They like to expand their vocabulary and are happy to look up a definition in a dictionary.

✻ They like when teachers have detailed notes.

Study tips best suited to the read/write learner

✻ Take plenty of notes, as the act of writing helps to reinforce the ideas and facts.

✻ Rewriting your notes in your own words is a very efficient way to cement the most important facts in your memory. However, writing out pages and pages of notes without learning, or even understanding, them is pointless.

* Have an organised colour-coded filing system in your folders for handouts, as handouts work well for the read/write learner.

* Most subjects lend themselves to bullet points. Condensing information into clear, easily remembered points helps the read/write learner.

* Diagrams, charts and graphs do not always appeal to the read/write learner, as they generally do not process information in this way. Compose short explanations for diagrams, graphs and charts. Add notes and subheadings to them so they are easier for you to remember.

* Focus in on key ideas and concepts using coloured highlighters and keep notes in the margin.

* Post-it notes stuck in visible areas help the read/write learner.

Strategies to help with studying

+ Mnemonic devices help students to simplify and remember challenging topics or large amounts of information. An image, a rhyme, an acronym or a phrase can help you to remember a list of facts in a certain order. For example, an **order mnemonic** for the lines on the music staff: Every Good Boy Deserves Food (E, G, B, D, F); an **acronym mnemonic** for the colours of the rainbow: Red, Orange, Yellow, Green, Blue, Indigo and Violet – Richard of York gave battle in vain; a **spelling mnemonic** for the word Rhythm: Rhythm Helps Your Two Hips Move; and a **rhyme mnemonic**: I before E except after C.

+ Mind-mapping helps us to think outside the box and can help to make information more accessible. A mind map is a visual summary of information which uses words, colours and pictures and connects related information using branches, so it resembles a tree. There are many wonderful websites online for mind-mapping, such as www.text2mindmap.com.

'Ask yourself if what you are doing today is getting you closer to where you want to be tomorrow.'

Unknown

✦ Try to expand your vocabulary by reading books, newspapers, articles and magazines. Write down the words you don't understand and look them up in a dictionary. Expanding your vocabulary allows you to express yourself in a more proficient and effective manner.

✦ Graphic Organisers are a visual method of organising, developing and summarising learning. They act like a scaffold for the construction of knowledge. They are beneficial for visual, auditory and kinaesthetic learners. The Irish Second Level Support Services (SLSS) funded by the Department of Education has an excellent Graphic Organiser booklet (find it at www.pdst.ie) which explains very clearly how to use all the different Graphic Organisers.

✦ Review what you have learned the day you learn it, and review it at different stages of the year after that. This is usually a much more effective method than cramming.

✦ When you are reading a comprehension piece, read the question first and try to highlight the key points and important information as you go along.

✦ If you feel that you are losing track of where you are on the page, use a ruler or index card to keep you focused.

'It always seems impossible until it is done.'

Nelson Mandela

✦ It is important to master the skills of organisation and time management, staying focused and developing the ability to see work through to the end. Keep assignments together in specific sections in folders and notebooks. We have noticed that girls often love to use bright, colourful folders – why not decorate your own? Make sure that you have a to-do list or a calendar to mark upcoming deadlines for school work and non-academic commitments so you can plan accordingly. This will help you to adjust to expectations, hence alleviating stress. Ensure that your study workspace is a distraction-free, orderly and well-lit area. Stick positive inspirational quotes up in your study space to keep you motivated!

✦ Something as simple as a checklist can really help. Prioritise your list so that you decrease your stress levels and feel more in control of your life. Your list should consist of manageable one-to-two-hour tasks. That way, you can focus your energy and effort on the task at hand without feeling overwhelmed. Crossing jobs off your checklist is a very satisfying experience – you can actually feel like a weight is being lifted from your shoulders as you do it. However, once you have completed something that has been weighing on you, it's essential that you reward yourself by doing something nice. The theory behind this is that activities that are followed by rewards generally become rewarding themselves. In time, you start to associate your study with positive consequences, which in turn motivates you. It's extremely difficult to participate in a productive study session if you're not feeling motivated. So find a healthy balance between leisure and study time.

✦ Some students feel that they do actually understand what they have learned but are unable to apply their knowledge to the exam questions. Is this you? If it is, remember that everything we do in life generally requires some form of practice. So, in this case, there really is no magic solution. Practise writing answers under pressure.

✦ Positive mental feedback sets up an expectation of success. Telling yourself that you are stupid or have a bad memory does nothing for your self-esteem and only escalates your stress. Tell yourself that you want to learn and believe that you can do it! Motivate yourself before you study, visualise and think of getting good grades, which will take you in the direction you need to go to get your dream job.

✦ The more we use our brain, the more it grows. In order to develop it, we can do some simple exercises like brushing our teeth or dialling phone numbers with our non-dominant hand. This is thought to activate the non-dominant side of our brain. Games like chess require us to use our grey matter while socially interacting and provide important stimulation.

✦ Try deep-breathing techniques and meditation before and after you study or before an exam. They can help you to relax. Cortisol, the stress hormone, can be harmful to memory if it is not relieved. Relaxation exercises, mindfulness and meditation can help you to remain calm.

✦ Try to exercise. Physical activity is not just good for toning your body – it also helps with concentration.

✦ Make an action board (see Chapter 16) to define goals in a creative way and to help keep you motivated and encouraged to do your best to stay on track.

'The secret to getting ahead is to get started.'

Mark Twain

✦ Before you start an essay, take a few minutes to write down an essay plan or a 'spider' plan. This will help you to lay out a well-structured answer and will also ensure that you keep to the point. Feeling as though you have a plan in place will also make it easier to begin – when you get stuck, just check your plan and move on to the next point.

✦ It is essential to eat well. A diet based on fruits, vegetables, wholegrains and healthy fats provides lots of health benefits and can also improve memory. B-vitamins, found in foods like spinach and most dark-green, leafy vegetables, play an important role in helping to protect neurons. Cognitive function has been associated with Omega-3 fatty acids, which are found in large amounts in the brain. They are thought to play an important role in concentration. The best sources of Omega-3 fatty acids are walnuts, cold-water fish and flax seeds.

✦ Sleep is essential when you are studying. Research suggests that sleep plays an important role in memory storage, both before and after learning a new task. It can be very difficult to concentrate when we do not get enough sleep.

✦ In the exam, take a few deep breaths to calm yourself before turning over your exam paper. If you do not immediately see a question you can answer, don't panic. Make a mind map or an essay plan to help you with brainstorming. Keep within the timeframe you have set for each question and try to leave a few minutes at the end, to check back over your answer.

✦ Get started. Like the famous anonymous quote says: 'Do it now. Sometimes "later" becomes "never".' If you are struggling to get motivated, focus on your long-term goals.

✦ Seize every opportunity you are given in life. Take hold of every occasion and make it great instead of waiting around for extraordinary opportunities. Perceive everything as an opportunity.

'Continuous effort – not strength or intelligence – is the key to unlocking our potential.'

Winston Churchill

Reducing stress

Chronic stress from academic pressure can affect our mental health, which in turn can lead to a negative downward spiral, resulting in higher anxiety levels and problems sleeping and retaining information.

(S): A student was putting extreme pressure on herself to get the best possible grades so that she could get the college course she wanted. She was also competing at a high level in a few sports. She often stayed up late to keep on top of things. She thought she had to manage it all by herself. Eventually, it all became too much, she was exhausted and had frequent headaches and stomach problems. She couldn't stay going. Once she sought help in school everything became more manageable. She has now learned to practise deep-breathing techniques which help her feel more grounded. She also listens to relaxation meditation CDs to reduce her stress. She feels more in control and can prioritise what's important.

Learn how to manage stress and live a balanced life. There are many techniques to prevent yourself from getting to this stage of stress overload, including relaxation, positive thinking, exercising, practising time management skills, communicating with family, friends and teachers and, most importantly, having a sense of humour.

Many people don't understand why they should become familiar with and practise relaxation techniques **before** they are feeling anxious. Do you wait until you need a filling to start brushing your teeth? Of course not. The same is true with academic stress. The more we practise stress-reducing techniques, the better we will be able to use them for intervention.

Career choices

Happiness is not in the mere possession of money;
it lies in the joy of achievement,
in the thrill of creative effort.'
Franklin D. Roosevelt

Choosing a career path can be confusing. While interest and passion are not the only requirements for feeling contented and rewarded in your career, they are very important. If you are really struggling with what career to choose, aim for a broader degree that will act as a stepping stone in the future. Doing this means that you can always study something more specific in your post-grad or master's. A chat with your career-guidance teacher can help to clear your mind and point you in the right direction. Research your chosen university online. Browse through the course outline, unit modules and career prospects. Go to open days, and ask plenty of questions. If you can, talk to university students studying your preferred subjects to determine if this is the right course for you. Talk with someone working in your field of interest and discuss their day-to-day activities or shadow someone for a few days to see if you still like it. If you make a wrong turn, don't panic: you are not lost; you are just taking the scenic route to your dream career. Your career is not a sprint but a marathon made up of your life experiences on a gently winding road.

We cannot control everything

We live in a world where we tend to reward perfectionists for setting high standards and we envy and admire their persistent drive to meet those standards. For some, the price they pay for success can be deep anxiety and chronic unhappiness.

Mistakes are proof that you are trying.

Aim high – but realise that everyone makes mistakes and that learning from them makes us even stronger. We all want to have control over what happens in our lives, but the reality is that there are many things outside of our control. Trying to manage every situation can raise our anxiety levels sky high. Mistakes, challenges and finding solutions are a part of life. It is better to fall flat on your face because you are trying, than to always play it safe and never know what you are capable of achieving. When you stumble and fall, you learn how to get up and avoid making the same mistakes as you venture on.

At times, we all worry and feel anxious, but energy spent worrying is futile. Worrying causes anxiety to grow and it drains us, both emotionally and physically. When you get anxious, ask yourself **'What is the worst that could happen?'** When you do, you realise that, firstly, the chances of the disaster striking is very slim and, secondly, if it did you could handle it.

'Only those who dare to fail greatly can ever achieve greatly.'

Robert F. Kennedy

If we let fear control us and never find the courage to take new opportunities, it is possible that we might spend the rest of our lives wondering what might have happened if we had only been a little bit braver.

Your best is good enough

In school you should try to not see your mistakes as personal flaws or failures. We all make them so use these blips to your advantage – learn from them and move on wiser and braver. Be persistent and consistent. Keep up to date with your study plans. Encourage, support and believe in yourself. Work to the best of your ability and remember – all you can do is your best.

Make your motto 'I will do the best I can, where I am, with what I have, now.'

Feeling Anxious

If we think about it, we would never talk to anyone the way we talk to ourselves. Stop for a moment and listen to some of the thoughts that often play over and over in your mind. 'I'm too fat.' 'I'm not popular.' 'I am beyond stupid at Maths.' Replace the word 'I' with 'you' and ask yourself how many friends you would have if you talked to them in this way.

Why are we so hard on ourselves?

'Research shows that perfectionism hampers success. In fact, it's often the path to depression, anxiety, addiction and life paralysis.'

Brené Brown, 'The Gifts of Imperfection'

We tend to be our own worst critics. Women can be extremely hard on both themselves and others. Nothing less than perfection will do, and often we feel profoundly dejected when we don't measure up. Why do we put ourselves through such torture? We tell ourselves that we are not smart enough, funny enough, interesting enough, pretty or slim enough and then wonder why we feel so bad. How can we lead fulfilled and happy lives if we are listening to this abuse all day every day? We are sabotaging our future happiness and our dreams. Many of us have become so used to the negative critic in our head that we never stop to think about the bad influence it is having on our lives. The good news is that we can control our thoughts if we put the work in and, if we try, we can become friends with ourselves. A change of perspective can fundamentally alter how we feel about ourselves.

Are you ready to take control of your life and tell those negative thoughts who is boss?

How do I become more positive and less anxious?

'It will never rain roses: when we want to have more roses, we must plant more roses.'

✿ George Eliot ✿

You are the director and screenwriter of your life. Maybe it's time to edit and rewrite your story …

The past is over – it is gone for good. Whatever happened there has little or no relevance to what is happening in your life today. It is your choice whether you want to remain chained to a past that is well and truly over or whether you decide that you deserve better. You can change your life today by changing the way that you think about yourself.

It is helpful, if you can manage it, to try and curb negative thinking as much as you can before you feel your anxiety is controlling you, rather than the other way around. If you are the type of person who feels anxious a lot, and many of us do, there are steps which you can take to help yourself to feel better.

TIPS TO AVOID NEGATIVE THINKING

✪ **There is no one else out there like you.** You actually have so much to offer if you sit down for a moment and think about it. Stop comparing yourself to other people and think for a second about what makes you different and a genuine original. There is not, nor ever has been, anyone like you on this planet. If you compare yourself to others you will never feel good enough. We are all making our way through life in the best way possible. Why not focus on your good qualities for a second and write them out on a piece of paper? Keep them somewhere nearby and look at this sheet every morning and especially when the old doubts and worries creep back for a visit. It's time to reboot or reprogramme your way of thinking. Accept yourself today just as you are. Stop telling yourself that you will be happy when you get all A's in your tests or when you lose a stone or when you are part of the interesting gang at school. Realise how fabulous you are now. What have you got to lose?

✪ **Never tell yourself that you should do something.** 'Should' is one word that should be eliminated from the English language! There is a lot of criticism lurking in this one little word. It implies that you are not quite good enough and won't be until you do what you are supposed to be doing. By using this word, we are sometimes setting impossibly high standards for ourselves. Who says how we should live our lives? Why do we always have to put pressure on ourselves? Fine, you have an important assignment due in next week – there is plenty of time to get it done but still you tell yourself that it should be done today. Why? A friend asks you to go to a party where you know there will be drugs – you don't want to go but feel that you should. Why? It's not only teens who have this dilemma on a regular basis but adults too. We all need to give ourselves a break.

There is nothing either good or bad but thinking makes it so.'

William Shakespeare, Hamlet'

✪ **Don't dig a hole for yourself.** Are you like many who have one bad experience and dwell on it until it magnifies and seems to consume you? When you focus on bad thoughts, chances are you will attract even more. Before you know it, all you seem to be thinking are negative thoughts that are increasing your sense of anxiety. We all know that our thoughts have a direct link to our feelings, so the more 'bad' thoughts we have, the worse we feel. If you find that you are having lots of negative thoughts, try to pull yourself back. **Negativity attracts more negativity**, so be very vigilant when it comes to your thought processes.

✪ **Do something that can change your mood.** If you feel your thoughts are becoming more negative and you feel anxious, do something which will help you to feel better – find a strategy that suits you. Go for a long, challenging run; call over to your best friend's house; have a playlist at hand crammed with uplifting, feel-good songs; watch a soppy movie with your mum. Do something, anything, to get you out of your own head for a little while. Invent a saying or mantra for yourself which you find soothing and calming. This approach may sound overly simplistic, but it's not. You will find that after a while, and surrounded by the right people, you can't help feeling better. It's all about getting out of a negative head space and into a more positive one. Remember, this all has a cumulative effect: the more you encourage yourself to be positive, the happier and healthier you become.

✪ **Leave the past where it belongs and stop worrying about the future.** The only thing we really have control over is the present moment. Nothing else really matters. Why then spend time regretting what we did or didn't do in the past? We replay distressing events from our past hoping to somehow make sense of them when all we are really doing is dragging those unpleasant times into our present. Likewise, fretting about an imagined future where things may or may not happen is equally futile. No one knows what is going to happen tomorrow, next week or even an hour from now.

(M) My father often told me when I was growing up that we spend most of our lives worrying about things that never even happen. I used to laugh at his home-spun wisdom but now I realise how right he was.

✪ Try to focus on what is happening **right now** in your life, even if it is uncomfortable. Observe how you are feeling in this moment. Try not to react to your feelings but look at them as an impartial observer would. By doing this, you take a lot of the charge out of negative emotions and thoughts. Be your own spiritual guide; tell yourself firmly that whatever you are thinking or even obsessing about is simply a thought and thoughts can be changed. When you are feeling anxious, ask yourself to stop whatever it is that you are doing and rate your feelings of anxiety from one to ten (ten being off-the-scale anxious). Ask yourself how you are feeling at that precise moment and mostly, if you really concentrate just on the moment in hand, you know that you are fine. It is really empowering when you acknowledge that all you ever have to deal with is **right now**. Everything else can wait.

The only thing we really have control over is the present moment.

Be your own best friend

Instead of criticising yourself when you are feeling anxious, be caring and protective. Imagine if your best friend came to you telling you that she felt scared and anxious. Would you mock and scorn her, telling her that she should be able to cope with whatever life is throwing at her? Of course not. You would most probably give her a big hug and tell her that it is OK to feel stressed and fearful. You would reassure her that no matter how bad she feels you will always be there for her. You need to treat yourself like your number one best friend. If this sounds bizarre to you, ask yourself: how do you treat yourself when things get difficult?

You will have to trust us here, but this really helps: whenever you get anxious, treat yourself like a little child. Ask yourself what you need right here, right now. If you need some time out or a bit of space from the hustle and bustle of life, make sure that you carve out some alone time where you can nurture yourself. Instead of deriding yourself for not feeling a hundred per cent, make the conscious choice to look after yourself until you feel better, no matter how long that takes. You may well find that once you take some of the pressure off yourself you will start to feel more relaxed. So the next time your heart starts beating at one hundred miles an hour and your palms get all sweaty and you feel wretched beyond belief, go to a quiet and safe place, sit down and **slowly** take at least five long, deep breaths and speak calmly and reassuringly to yourself. Tell yourself to sit with the anxious feelings, let them simply wash over you. Repeat the following phrase as many times as you need to: **'this will pass'**. The natural reaction is to fight anxiety by ignoring it (which, let's face it, is impossible) or by 'forcing' ourselves out of it, which only serves to increase the feelings of fear and dread.

Sit with whatever emotions are engulfing you and remember that they are only emotions and in time they **will** vanish and new ones will take their place. The first time you do this you will feel out of your depth but the more you practise this, you will notice that not only has the anxiety less of a hold on you but also you are actually the master of your own mind.

You are in control of your thoughts.

The more you do this, the more you will realise how strong you actually are. The nicer and more nurturing you are to yourself when you are feeling scared, the less hold anxiety will have on you.

(M): Recently, in a senior English class, we watched a speech given by Bressie in the Bord Gáis Energy Theatre in Dublin. In it, he talked openly and frankly and very humorously about how he has battled crippling anxiety since his early teens. He recounted how debilitating anxiety left him feeling, saying that his life was almost ruined by the condition. I have to say, I was extremely impressed by him because he managed to talk about anxiety in a way that my students could relate to. Looking around my classroom, I could see that the eighteen-year-olds were listening to every word he said. Anxiety unfortunately is a common complaint in Ireland among people of all ages. It is time that all of us – adults and teens – started talking about it.

Bressie mentioned that for years he simply crumbled every time he felt a panic attack coming on (he said that he had one every night at 2 a.m. for years). He got so tired of it that he started to pull back from his life. One night, something cracked; he had an epiphany of sorts and he decided there and then to do something about it. So he picked a name for his anxiety – he called it Jeffrey. He decided to take Jeffrey on in his own inimitable way. As he is an athlete, he decided that he would beat Jeffrey by out-running him. When the 'panic attacked' every night, he jumped out of bed, like a man possessed, and ran through the streets of his home town until Jeffrey decided to call it a night and disappear! Eventually, the attacks lessened. This was Bressie's way of dealing with anxiety and it worked for him. The reason why I'm including this story here is that he decided to do something about his anxiety; he decided that he was in control and it was time to fight back.

I think in Ireland, at long last, that we are finally beginning to open up about anxiety in a way that, say, my parents' generation never could. People like Ray D'Arcy and Donal Walsh have definitely helped because they talked about mental health freely and sensibly. Teenagers today are anxious but they are also willing to talk about how they feel if they are presented with a safe platform where they can do so.

Anxiety is very common. We all know people who, at some stage in their lives, have experienced it. However, to look at them from the outside, one would never, even for a second, suspect that anything was wrong. Life today can throw all sorts of curve balls and difficulties at us and sometimes, not always, this can make us lose our balance. Anxiety is treatable: it is not, nor does it have to be, a lifetime condition. If you feel that anxiety is taking over your life and you cannot seem to manage it alone, don't suffer in silence. Talk to a parent, a friend or someone who can help.

'Man is free at the moment he wishes to be.'

❧ Voltaire ❧

Panic attacks

If you are experiencing anxiety, you may find that you have become irritable, detached and angry, and your parents and friends might notice a change in your disposition. Talk to them; don't isolate yourself and the people you love at this difficult time. Also, you may need to enlist the help of a professional who can help you deal with what is happening. With the right advice, you can not only manage the attacks but also say goodbye to them forever.

(S) A student once told me that when she first started getting panic attacks she thought she was going to choke. She was afraid all of the time and there were times when she felt as if everything and everyone posed a threat. Now, after getting help, she knows that all anyone can do is their best and that this is always enough. Mindfulness helped her to realise that all she needed to control is now and this gave her a huge sense of relief. Before she got help she was very hard on herself, so critical. She would urge anyone suffering from anxiety to go easier on themselves and be more nurturing and compassionate. Anxiety is a condition that can be treated very successfully. She was consumed by fear, believing that she was condemned to a life filled with fear and panic attacks. This is not the case – you can get help. Now whenever she gets anxious she is able to practise coping strategies that allow her to live a full and happy life, because she knows now that life really is for living.

> You can beat this, starting today.

How to deal with panic attacks

Do you know what works for you when you feel an attack coming on? Are you afraid that you will have an attack in school? Have you told your parents and your closest friends about how you are feeling?

When a panic attack strikes, adrenaline floods your body. As a result, you may feel a total lack of control and be absolutely terrified. This is perfectly normal. It is important at the outset to remind yourself that no matter how frightening the attack is, and no matter how bad you feel, **a panic attack cannot actually harm you in any way**. Even though your heart is racing, your palms are sweating and you are afraid that you might be losing your mind, stop and register the following facts:

✦ Panic attacks are extremely common: you are not alone.

✦ While you may be having difficulty breathing and catching your breath and your heart might feel like it is jumping out of your chest, it won't. You are **not** having a heart attack.

✦ Your mind may be racing and you might be afraid that you are losing control. Tell yourself **over and over** that panic cannot actually harm you. Having panic attacks does not mean that you have a mental health issue. Remind yourself of this fact as often as you need to.

When you feel an attack coming on, your first instinct may be to try to run away from it and the unpleasant feelings. This is completely understandable but this actually could be adding to the intensity of the attack and making it worse rather than better. Research shows that the best thing to do is to sit or lie down, making the body completely still. Now if you are in school you cannot lie down but you could put your head on your desk. Better still, ask permission to leave the classroom, go to the toilet and sit or lean up against the wall for **as long as it takes**.

Breathe slowly, even if this is very difficult to do. Breathe in and out. Do this over and over until you can feel your body and your breathing becoming calmer. It can be comforting to put your hand on your stomach while doing this. Breathing slowly sends a message to your brain that you are now in control. You can do this but it takes courage and patience. Repeat over and over, '**This will pass**.' Let the fear and anxiety wash over you like a wave on the beach. By doing this, you are telling your mind that you are not in any danger, even though it may feel like you are.

I breathe in love and light – I breathe out panic and fear.

Think safe, comforting thoughts. Tell yourself that this attack is just temporary; it will be over soon. Attacks usually last between five and twenty minutes. Remind yourself that, as horrible as they are, the attacks won't actually harm you or your health.

Emergency drill for panic attacks

✦ Go somewhere that you feel safe.

✦ Avoid the inclination to run and hide.

✦ Sit still. Place your hand on your stomach and breathe in deeply.

✦ Breathe in and out, letting the fear wash over you.

✦ Comfort yourself by repeating, 'This will pass.'

✦ Before you know it, it will.

The more times that you manage to sit calmly with yourself and let the attack break over you, the stronger you will get. The first time you do this is obviously the hardest, but each time after, the panic lessens its grip a little. Make sure to give yourself credit for being brave enough and calm enough to sit through an attack. Bit by bit, the balance of power will shift, as you will start to control your panic rather than the other way around.

Take care, breathe deeply and surrender. Every time you deal with panic in this way, you will feel stronger and stronger, as you realise that you are doing something to make yourself more relaxed. Believe that you can control and master these attacks and you will.

'Dwell on the beauty of life. Watch the stars and see yourself running with them.'

Marcus Aurelius

Eyes Wide Open

So many times, especially in the run-up to important exams, students tell us how they are having trouble getting to sleep at night. As adolescents need more sleep than adults do (between eight and a half and nine hours), this sleeplessness can cause them considerable distress. Many have confessed that they find it difficult to sleep at night no matter how tired they feel physically. As a result, they often find it hard to concentrate the next day in school. This only serves to increase the levels of stress and anxiety that they are feeling.

Remember, different people need different things – we don't all need eight hours of sleep a night. What is important is the **quality** of sleep that you manage to get and how good or bad you feel after a night's rest. Are you feeling overwhelmed at school? Are things building up in your mind?

Is sleeplessness an issue?

'Sleep is the best meditation.'
Dalai Lama

Ask yourself the following questions if you suspect that sleep or sleeplessness is becoming an issue for you.

✳ Does it take you absolutely ages to fall asleep at night? Do you go to bed early only to find that you are wide awake hours later, when the rest of the house is sleeping soundly?

✳ Do you feel exhausted, moody and irritable during the day at school?

✳ Do you wake up many times during the night?

✳ Do you find it difficult to go back to sleep once you have woken up?

✳ Do you wake up a few hours too early in the morning and, despite your best efforts, find that you cannot drift off to sleep again?

You need to be very honest with yourself. Is there anything that you are doing during the day that might be preventing you from resting properly at night time? What about the obvious – are you drinking a lot of tea and coffee during the day? If so, try to limit your intake significantly for a while and never drink caffeine after lunchtime, as it could be a factor to consider. If you are going through a period of sleeplessness, the tendency is to worry about sleeping. Of course, this only makes insomnia worse.

One day a student told us how in the past she always went to bed with her phone in her hand, looking at Facebook, Instagram and Snapchat before plugging it in to charge beside her bed. Then she would try to fall asleep … and try … and try. She was exhausted and had frequent headaches. Eventually a visiting speaker in school told the girls that there is a link between the light emitting from screens and our circadian rhythms (often referred to as our body clock). The speaker said that screens contain a great deal of blue light which has a stimulating effect on the body. The students also learned that charging anything beside their head is not beneficial because the charger plugged into the mains could be giving off an electro-magnetic field. She now keeps her bedroom free of mobile phones and other electronic devices and is sleeping much better. She now knows that if you need to switch off, switch your phone off first.

So here are a few tips to help get you through this frustrating phase.

TIPS TO HELP YOU SLEEP

✪ If you find yourself tossing and turning for hours on end, try to assure yourself that your body **will give in** and fall asleep when it absolutely needs to. Try not to worry about the next day, which is out of your control anyway, and instead focus your attention on calming the mind. Tell yourself that even though you are not sleeping now, you accept, love and approve of yourself anyway. Focus on how you are feeling and breathing now. Chances are that once you slow the breath down, place your hands on your stomach and observe your thoughts without judging them, you will feel better. Practising mindfulness really helps when dealing with insomnia. As you are concentrating on the breath coming in and going out, you naturally quieten the mind and still the soul. A lovely affirmation to use here is 'I breathe in calm and I exhale any worrying thoughts, stress and fears.'

(M): I read a fantastic book recently by Dr Joseph Murphy called *The Power of Your Subconscious Mind*. According to him, we need to take control of our subconscious mind, i.e. the thoughts that we are unaware of, and let the rational mind tell it what to think. He claims that the subconscious mind is like a little child, one who needs to be taken by the hand and instructed as to what to do and think. If we don't guide it, Murphy claims, chaos and a lack of control could ensue. So, to cut a long story short, you need to tell your subconscious mind before you go to sleep every night that you will sleep beautifully from now on. Try this technique out the next time you find yourself worrying about a bad night's sleep or how tiredness might affect you the next day.

✪ Your sleeplessness could be a sign that you are worried or anxious about some area of your life. Ask yourself what is **preoccupying** you at the moment. Is life, school or a relationship causing you difficulty? What about writing down what is on your mind? Often, while lying awake at night, we tend to dramatise our problems. Usually, when you write down what is bothering you in the cold light of day, and when you look at what you have written, often it just does not seem as bad as it did at two in the morning. We need to learn how to be compassionate with ourselves. Instead of scolding yourself for not sleeping, you should nurture yourself and be even nicer to yourself than you usually are. Why not make a worry box? Write down all of your worries and problems, fold the page and pop it into the worry box. It helps with establishing what is wrong. Alternatively, write any worries on a blank page and burn it, letting them go once and for all.

✪ Establish and follow a relaxing bedtime routine. An hour or so before you retire for the night, make yourself a hot cup of milk or herbal tea. Having a hot bath with some essential oils is a lovely way to switch off.

✪ Turn off your tablet, TV or phone – even better still, keep them out of your bedroom altogether. These only over-stimulate the mind, which is the last thing you want before nodding off for the night. So forget about everybody in the outside world – they can contact you in the morning. And remember: leave all devices downstairs and out of reach.

✪ Other things can cause insomnia. Make sure that your bedroom is not too hot, cold or bright. Try to associate your bedroom with sleeping and relaxation and not work. Cold and flu, headaches or other physical ailments can make sleeping difficult. To feel reassured, remind yourself that this is simply a short-term problem and it will pass in time.

✪ **Try not to worry too much**. Remember, everyone has problems sleeping from time to time. If the problem is persisting, however, be sure to enlist the help of parents and loved ones and you may want to pay your doctor a visit. Remember: never be afraid to ask for help.

I have done my best today, my body deserves
a restful sleep.

✪ Try to stick to a regular sleep schedule. I know this sounds difficult, but support your body by going to bed and getting up at the same time **every** day. It is tempting to stay in bed longer at the weekends in order to make up for lost time but this only interferes with your biological clock and causes more disturbances. Do not sleep for twelve hours straight on a Saturday night only to find yourself tossing and turning on the Sunday night. Be strict with yourself.

✪ Avoid arguments or intense phone conversations before bedtime. These can cause worry and interfere with your sleep. Focus instead on relaxing, soothing activities.

✪ Even though you may want to, do not look at the time in the middle of the night. This will make you worry about your performance the next day even more. Step away from the alarm clock! Trust me on this one. Let go, accept and breathe.

> 'Sleep that knits up the ravelled sleeve of care
> The death of each day's life, sore labour's bath
> Balm of hurt minds, great nature's second course,
> Chief nourisher in life's feast.'
> ✧ William Shakespeare, 'Macbeth' ✧

It might help if you ask and answer these questions:

✦ What problems specifically do you have? Do you wake up in the middle of the night or too early in the morning and then find that, no matter what, you cannot go back to sleep? Or do you have trouble falling asleep?

✦ What is stressing you out in your life at the moment? Have you recently had a big falling-out with a friend or partner? Is schoolwork getting on top of you? Is there anything happening at home that is worrying you? Think about this and write your thoughts in a journal or diary.

✦ Are you the worrying type? Are you the sort of person who worries when you are not worrying?

✦ Is there an event that occurred when you were young that could be re-running itself in your mind now, years later? Decide upon a time where you will practise relaxation or mindfulness and promise yourself that you will stick to it.

> **I now choose to clear my mind of all thoughts and relax into a deep sleep.**

✦ What benefit is there to staying up half the night wide awake? Even though you feel physically very tired, it can be very difficult to turn off your mind in the middle of the night. Do you find your mind jumping from one idea to the next? This is called monkey mind and it can prevent you from getting a good night's sleep. Give yourself permission to put all your worries aside for the night; they can wait until the morning. An affirmation which is nice to use before you fall asleep is 'I bless the day and release it now; I am falling into a restful sleep knowing that tomorrow will take care of itself.' Repeat this phrase until you can actually feel your mind and body letting go.

Have patience with yourself. Remember, you are reprogramming your mind. It is as if you have got a giant hoover and are sucking all the fearful and negative thoughts out of your mind and replacing them with positive, nurturing ones. Worrying is a habit; it is a choice. You don't have to do it. You can change your thoughts but you have to be willing to put in the effort.

Lastly, please don't let a bout of insomnia bring you down. Remember, the more attention you give it, the greater a part it will play in your life. **It will pass**. You need to remind yourself of that every day. Also, it won't kill you! Instead of feeling sorry for yourself, remind yourself of all the good things in your life – for example, family and friends. You are a wonderful, special individual. You can still lead a great life even though you may be having trouble temporarily with sleep. Focus on the positive, practise all the tips above and rest happy.

Sweet dreams!

When Time Stands Still

We are all complicated individuals who feel, think, act and react to life in our own particular and unique ways. When a loved one is seriously ill, teenagers can feel overwhelmed by loss and bewilderment and may not know where to turn.

'Courage is not having the strength to go on, it is going on when you don't have the strength.'

⁓ Theodore Roosevelt ⁓

Dealing with critical illness

This is a confusing and difficult time. Of course you feel worried but, if you can manage it, do not allow these feelings to overwhelm you. It is perfectly acceptable to ask questions and express exactly how you feel, even if you think that you should protect your loved ones by hiding your sadness, fear or anger.

Let others support you. You do not have to go through this challenging time alone. Family and friends want to be there for you. It can really help you to cope when you release and share your concerns with others. Getting a new perspective can provide clarity and will help you to understand this difficult situation a little better. Even though your loved one probably has less energy to do all the things that you previously enjoyed doing together, they still love the ground you walk on. Spend time with them so that you can continue to create special memories which you will cherish in the years to come.

It can be hard to know exactly what to say to your loved one but by listening you are being more supportive than you will ever know. Having said that, try not to pressurise them to talk about their illness when they are not willing or able to. Of course you want to help, but sometimes you may not know how to. If you are anxious, try asking them honest and simple questions such as 'What can I do to help?' or 'What do you need today?'

Believe it or not, you still need to have fun and spend time with your friends. You may feel disloyal to your loved one when you decide to go out with your friends. Do not feel guilty about this. Continue to live your life.

(S): I can still vividly remember a student asking me 'Is there a correct way to grieve – what should I be doing?' No therapist or self-help book can predict what a teenager will go through on the grief journey because it is a different experience for each one of us. Sorrow changes in character and intensity over time and how long each person spends grieving is entirely up to them. That said, facing grief head-on can be more constructive than holding pain inside. Some teens may fall into complicated grieving patterns which are destructive and are often an attempt to temporarily numb the pain.

Coping with grief and loss as a teenager

Following the death of a loved one, grief is a very natural part of the process of trying to come to terms with this major change in your life. You may well find that you want to resist or reject your grief but it is important not to ignore it. Shedding a few tears can do wonders to help you get through it all. People want to help you. You do not have to feel sad all of the time – it is acceptable to laugh and feel happy when you want to. Do not feel guilty when you momentarily forget your pain and find yourself laughing out loud at a funny comment that a friend makes or a comic scene from your favourite TV programme. It just means that your wounds are **slowly** beginning to heal. Every November in our school we hold a memorial service. The students find that it helps them to deal with grief and loss. The theme for the service in 2014 was based around the beautiful Eskimo proverb 'Perhaps they are not stars, but rather openings in heaven, where the love of our lost ones pours through and shines down upon us to let us know they are happy.'

Grief is a very powerful and necessary emotion; it allows us to be honest with our feelings and helps us to find closure. In the words of Earl Grollman, 'Grief is not a disorder, a disease or a sign of weakness. It is an emotional, physical and spiritual necessity, the price you pay for love. The only cure for grief is to grieve.'

A word of warning – becoming consumed with grief long-term can undo your sense of balance in life.

(M): After the tragic death of a loved one, a student came to me – she began by saying things like 'If only I had said or done' or 'If only I had known' or 'I should have been there more for him.' I explained to her that she could not change the past, but that she must accept that every moment of her life was based on her circumstances at that time, that she did the best she could based on what she believed and was capable of.

No matter how much we may wish to turn back time, we know in our heart of hearts that we cannot. Somehow, we must let go of the fear of facing the future without our loved one. We all ask questions after an untimely death. If you can, let go of the guilt of having said or done something that you may now regret. Below are some techniques that can help with the grieving process.

Mindfulness meditation

Mindfulness meditation helps to facilitate healing. It allows us to help clear our minds and refocus our thoughts so that when grief's tidal wave hits us with force, we have the ability to keep our bodies calm and grounded.

Affirmations

Think wisely when choosing your thoughts; address and try to change the areas where you cannot find peace. Focus on love rather than loss. Instead of focusing on how much you cherished and adored your loved one while they were alive, remember that you can continue to love them even in their absence. Some sample affirmations are:

- 'I feel my grief but I refuse to wallow in it.'
- 'I choose to focus on the wonderful memories we shared and the love we felt for each other. I will never forget you.'

Journaling

The beauty of journaling is that there are no rules, so you can just write whatever you feel. When you are adjusting to death and its accompanying feelings of loss and despair, it can be consoling and comforting to record your movement through it. Writing unsent letters is uplifting and an effective way to say things that were left unsaid between you. Picture yourself in the future thriving and surviving. In your journal, write about how you imagine yourself coping in one year's time. It can speed up your progress and help you to move gently towards the healing side of grief.

Relaxation

After the loss of a loved one, it is not always just our heart that suffers but our whole body. Grief can manifest itself in many ways such as exhaustion, nausea or shortness of breath. Practising relaxation exercises can help your entire body to unwind and it also helps your mind to find rest. Listening to natural sounds like ocean waves can also help you to relax, as you picture your grief being washed away with the waves. Do this for five minutes and gradually, if you can, increase it.

Grief can feel like a backpack filled with a heavy load, but in due course, it will lighten until you arrive at a day in the future when it is barely noticeable. Gradually, the positive times will increase, until grief no longer controls every aspect of your life. Eventually you will be able to quietly honour your loved one, whom you still miss so much. You may even be able to support others who are coping with grief. A friend of ours who lost her father to cancer last year has turned her sadness into a constructive project and has published a hugely successful celebrity cookbook, *Food for Thought*, to raise funds for cancer support. Mindfulness and meditation are tools that helped her and can help you arrive at that place too.

Two Halves Still
Make a Whole

During adolescence you are looking for more independence, testing boundaries and trying to work out who you really are. It is possible that you are looking to your parents to see how a romantic relationship should be. What do you do then if their marriage is falling apart in front of your eyes? Do you feel that your needs are not being met because your mum and dad are preoccupied with their own issues and emotions? Please remember – they are not trying to hurt you: they are just trying to process their own feelings, make it through the whirlwind and come out the other side. It is very possible that they are distracted and confused but, remember, they will always love you – no matter what.

Everyone reacts differently to separation or divorce: some philosophical students will accept it, while others are sad, angry, frustrated, confused and wish to lash out. There are those who want to stay at home all of the time, while others feel that they need to escape from the home environment, preferring to spend time with their friends. If your parents decide to go their separate ways, and you are fretting about how this is going to affect you, do not worry about being selfish. However, try to be considerate about their feelings too.

Have faith that things will work out. Maybe not as you planned, but how it's meant to be.

The emotional stresses of a family break-up

(S): Some years ago, a student told me about how burdened she felt because her parents were constantly confiding in her and she talked about how difficult things were since they split. She was afraid that she too was destined to fail at love.

No matter how mature you may appear or act, you should never have to carry the weight of mature, adult conversations. No one wants to hear all the unpleasant details about their parents' relationship. After a break-up, parents themselves may be feeling sad and lonely and need a shoulder to cry on. Of course these emotions are important to express, but not with you – you are still the child; they are the adults.

If you are feeling overburdened, explain clearly to your parents that you will still love and support them, but that you cannot and will not shoulder the responsibility of 'fixing' their sadness.

(M): Once, a student approached me explaining how she felt that her parents were using her as a scapegoat. She felt caught in the middle of their rage and disappointment. I asked her to explain that she loved them both dearly and did not want to have to choose between them, or hear undesirable gossip about either of them. She did have to repeat this message a few times before her needs were recognised. I suppose what is important to remember here is that boundaries are not only necessary but healthy. Refuse point blank to relay messages, carry stories or worse still, take sides. In the long-run, this will benefit everyone.

Your parents are separating from each other, not from you

Try to have regular contact with the parent that you are not living with. Just say hello, give them a call and keep them informed about what is happening in your life. Your mum and dad may have fallen out of love with each other, but they still want to be a part of your life even if they live under a different roof and in a different town. You may have to face the challenge of travelling between parents. If so, ask your parents to maturely handle visiting arrangements. Some girls think that the divorce is somehow their fault and feel guilty about what has happened. Try to remember that your parents' separation is a result of their own problems with each other, not with something that you said or did.

The reality is that people can change, relationships may not always last forever and it can be much more damaging for children to live in a chaotic home with two adults trying to make a struggling marriage work than to move on.

> I know my parents are separating from one another, not from me.

TIPS TO HELP ADJUST TO A SEPARATION

✪ At times, teenagers find it hard to forgive their parents after a split, as they feel that their world has been turned upside down. Your parents are most likely doing the best they can in difficult circumstances. Feeling anger and rage is like holding a burning log: the only person getting burnt is you. You have to learn to forgive everyone involved so that healing can take place. If possible, relax and let the hurt go.

✪ After a marital break-up, stress can present in many different ways. For some, it can feel like your body muscles are really tightening up. Practise techniques that can calm and soothe you. Without the ability to relax, we can drain all of our energy with negative emotions.

✪ Belly breathing can really help you to feel better. Learn to focus on your breath. Sit in a comfortable position with one hand on your stomach and close your eyes. Focus on your breathing. As you inhale, allow your belly to expand. Think about your lungs inflating. Slowly exhale and picture your body relaxing. Visualise your lungs deflating and your breath releasing all tension. Allow your belly to flatten. If your mind starts to wander, calmly try to refocus and turn your attention back to your breath. This kind of breathing can really help to settle your nerves. It also helps you to relax before sleeping.

The truth is that things are going to be different. It is hard for you, but in time, hopefully, you will see that your parents are happier apart, which in turn could lead to your relationship with them being even better than before. Teens often surprise themselves after a parental split. Learning to cope with difficult circumstances can help you later in life. Keep your eye on the positive things in your life and you will get through this admirably.

> I still love my parents and they will always love me.
> I can make it through this and be happy.

Part Two

Taking Control of Your Destiny

Achieving Happiness

Moving forward in life with positive thinking gives you a better outlook. Life can be tough but we need to realise that it is a gift. In the words of Marcus Aurelius, 'When you arise in the morning, think of what a precious privilege it is to be alive – to breathe, to think, to enjoy, to love.' Learn to tune in to the positive. We all have internal conversations like 'I will be happy when …' Maybe it is time to change this talk. We tell ourselves that we cannot possibly change, but if we are open to the possibility of happiness we can do anything.

(M): In early 2015, I was lucky enough to go to Cork's city hall for the Young Social Innovators Speak-Out. There, I witnessed transition-year students from all over Ireland telling the judges and the audience how they would like to change the world for the better and explaining through song, dance and mime why they picked the social issue that their projects were based on. My group wanted to focus on happiness. For three weeks they were like happiness fairies, flying around the corridors making sure that everyone who came into contact with them left feeling a little lighter and more joyous. The one thing that I learned from the girls is that, yes, happiness really is contagious! Here's an excerpt from their speech:

'Everybody hurts. Depression, stress and loneliness affect all of us at some stage in our lives. Our project is called The Pursuit of Happiness. We want to tackle negative vibrations and promote positive mental health. We are here to remind you that broken crayons still colour.

Happiness comes from looking at what you have, not what is missing. Some days, you just have to create your own sunshine – not because everything is good, but because you can see the good in everything. Small gestures can make a difference. Surround yourself with the dreamers and the doers but, most of all, surround yourself with people who can see the greatness in you when you cannot see it yourself.'

We have all looked at people who radiate good energy and happiness and wished desperately that we could be just like them. These people are true optimists; they shine from the inside out. Having this attitude helps us to get what we want out of life while having fun at the same time.

Everyone falls over along the way. Dwelling on issues solves nothing. Accept your mistakes and move on. There is always a solution to any problem. Here are some strategies to help with positivity.

TIPS FOR STAYING POSITIVE

✪ **Clear negativity.** Why not change your negative statements into positive ones? Say 'I always find a way to solve my problems.' Negative beliefs cloud our vision and only trick and deceive us into holding back. They do not reinforce the greatness that is inside each one of us and they prevent you from seeing the intended journey of your life clearly.

✪ **Practise gratitude.** Gratitude works. Focus on all the good things that you have in your life, rather than concentrating only on what you do not have. Like the saying goes, we have to find the good in our bad and the happy in our sad.

> There is always, always, always something to be thankful for.

✪ **Surround yourself with interesting and supportive people.** Being around optimistic, funny and energetic people will bring about positive results in your life. Negative people drain us of energy, making us tired and exhausted. They are like the Dementors in *Harry Potter* or the Black Riders in *The Lord of the Rings*. They take all the beauty and vitality out of life and leave us with nothing but a vague feeling of dissatisfaction. Joyful people and their loving presence nurture and encourage us. If we are positive we will attract positive people and situations. When it rains, look for rainbows. Believe that everything is possible. In the words of Audrey Hepburn: 'Nothing is impossible; the word itself says I'm possible.'

- ✪ **Be responsible for your own actions.** Remind yourself every day that although you may not be able to control what happens to you all of the time, you are always in charge of your **reaction** to situations. This is important! Keep repeating, 'I am in charge of how I feel and today I am choosing happiness and joy.' When you get up every morning, put your right foot on the ground first and say, 'I am starting today on the right foot.' Your subconscious mind is powerful. If you begin your day with a negative attitude, it can quickly spiral into a negative whirl. Every time you think a dark and depressing thought, replace it with a positive one to keep your body and mind in a nice state of balance and harmony. When you are having a bad day, remember that it is just one day, and it doesn't mean that all of your days will be bad.

- ✪ **Turn 'I can't' into 'I really can!'** Examine the way you phrase sentences. Instead of saying 'I always get a bad result in my Biology test, I just cannot do it', why not say, 'OK, that exam might not have worked out the way I had hoped, but I know I can improve and, next time, my result **will** be better.' Make a **real** effort to see challenges as opportunities, and prepare to be pleasantly surprised as doors open up where there were none before.

- ✪ **Accept yourself.** Your self-esteem will grow as soon as you stop being so hard on yourself and accept yourself for who you are. Self-acceptance is crucial to happiness and well-being.

- ✪ **Stop trying to change others.** Life becomes more peaceful when you accept that everyone is an individual and has their own point of view. We all see life from our own perspective. You do not need another's approval to be happy.

- ✪ **Forgive.** As we go through life, there will be times when we will experience pain, injury or betrayal. Initially, we may feel hurt but sometimes the sensation lingers on too long. Holding a grudge against a person only causes us to further injure ourselves. It takes courage to let go of these feelings when you have been wronged in some way. Forgiveness can heal the heart. It does not mean that you are forgetting the past: it just means that you are letting go and moving on.

○ **Be kind.** If you can, avoid being judgemental. Stop gossiping, otherwise you will never make progress. Being kind means giving yourself and others the benefit of the doubt instead of expecting perfection. If you are having a rotten day, don't be afraid to express your feelings in a kind way instead of bottling them up. A good cry can do wonders for the soul.

○ **Set your own standards.** Become the captain of your own ship. Decide who you want to be and what you want to achieve and accomplish, instead of worrying about what other people think of you and trying to live up to their expectations. Write down ten of your favourite things to do and try to arrange to do one of them this week.

○ **Remember to laugh.** Having a sense of humour can make all the difference. Whatever you do, be able to laugh at yourself. Laughter is a powerful antidote to stress and pain. Humour lightens our burdens and connects us with others. Laughing at ourselves and making others laugh helps to create an optimistic mind-set and is a very attractive quality. Look for the humour in a bad situation and uncover the absurdity and irony of life.

○ **Create a positive environment at home.** Hang up inspirational or funny posters all around the house. Frame photos of yourself, your family and friends having a blast. Choose a computer screensaver that makes you smile. Take down **anything** that lowers your mood. Be ruthless about this. Only accept the positive. Make a conscious decision to have more fun.

○ **Smile.** Smiling not only makes us look more attractive but it is actually good for our health. A happy, positive expression will serve you well in life.

○ **Spend time with friends.** Where, oh where, would we be without them? Friends help us to celebrate good times and they support us during the bad days. Rejoice in each other's successes.

✪ **Dance away your worries.** Dancing is a super form of exercise because it helps to build muscle and burn calories. All exercise releases endorphins but dancing has an increased effect on us because of the way music affects the mind. Music lifts our mood. So, turn up Ed Sheeran, dance like no one is watching and shake off any feelings of negativity. Alternatively, compile a playlist with your favourite songs.

✪ **Be helpful.** Volunteering and helping others enhances our motivation to feel better about ourselves by giving us a sense of community.

✪ **Get organised and manage your time well.** When we are organised we are calmer and happier. Ensure that your study workspace is a distraction-free, orderly and well-lit area and not a bomb site which your mother only enters when she really has to. Turn off your phone to avoid distraction. Complete the sentence 'I feel happy when …'

✪ Instead of focusing on what you cannot do or what you do not have, look at the bigger picture. Don't get discouraged. We all have days when we feel a little sad and blue. However, long-term, it is important that you strive for positivity on a daily basis. When you feel lonely or disheartened try to implement some of the above tips. Gradually, you **will** feel happier, we promise!

'Happiness depends upon ourselves.'

Aristotle

Action Boards –
Creating Your Dream Future

Sometimes it can be difficult to capture what we want from life. Our heads can be crammed with thoughts and dreams, yet we haven't a clue how to make them happen. Action boards help us to create a visual expression of our goals. They can keep us motivated and encourage us to do our best and to stay on track. In essence, they are a success plan in a visual format.

The problem is that many people wish and dream but do not take action. With an action board you do not just visualise your goals by cutting out pictures, as you do with a vision board. An action board is slightly different because it requires you to actually **do** something which will make your dreams become a reality. Positive thinking about your future is beneficial, but it must involve pragmatic planning and not just fantasising. As Dr Joseph Mercola (www.mercola.com) said, 'Your consistent thoughts become reality, dreams don't necessarily come true but they do take you in directions.'

We all dream in pictures or images. Images are the language of the unconscious mind. Our conscious mind is also very affected by them, which is why advertisers use images to influence us. When you use powerful goal-oriented images on your action board, they can help to influence you. Students have said that their action boards made them feel empowered and helped them to stay focused on what was important to them. Seeing the images of their dream job, car or university inspired them to keep striving to fulfil their dreams.

'We did not come to fear the future,
we came here to shape it.'
Barack Obama

An action board is like a collage of pictures – it depicts clearly all the things that you want to get from life. You can use magazine cut-outs, printed images, drawings, photos or any other affirmations or positive quotes that remind you of your goals. The idea is that you bring about positive change by focusing your mind on things and situations which you want to achieve in your life.

'Our aspirations are our possibilities.'

Robert Browning

Over the next few days or weeks get busy. Gather images, affirmations and quotations that represent your vision. Some people prefer to create scrapbook versions as they are more private. However, keep it accessible and visible, as if it is out of sight it may go out of mind.

By taking positive action you will see positive results.

How do I start imagining and creating my dream future?

✳ All you need is a scissors, glue, images and a large sheet of card or a scrapbook and a wild imagination!

✳ Organise the order of the images before you stick them on your board.

✳ Once you have completed your vision board you should make a corresponding action plan. **Work out how you will make your vision materialise.** Write down achievable steps or statements. For example, if one of your goals is to get in shape, you might either stick a picture of yourself at your ideal weight or a picture of somebody you admire at a healthy weight. Your action plan would then be to eat better food, drink more water and reduce your intake of junk food. You would also try to exercise and try to meditate more.

Review your action board regularly. By doing this, you keep your goals fresh in your mind. All of the positive sayings, words and pictures will keep you committed and motivated to keep going. I personally look at one of the positive sayings on my board every morning when I am getting ready and keep it in my mind throughout the day.

> A positive thought in the morning can change your whole day.

'Go confidently in the direction of your dreams.
Live the life you've imagined.'
Henry David Thoreau

Attitudes of Gratitude

Every morning, the minute you open your eyes and realise that you're in the land of the living, why not say thank you for all the good things in your life, those things that add colour to your world and which make your life worthwhile. So, before you contemplate getting out of bed tomorrow, why not list off your family, even if they drive you crazy, your wonderful friends, your dog, your health (even if you feel lousy) and your school, even if you just want to stay at home in your pyjamas watching *Homeland*. Doing this can actually put you in a positive frame of mind for the rest of the day.

If we are positive and happy, good things will come our way.

Gratitude is seriously underrated. We live in a world where people love to moan about all the things that are going wrong – whether it is the weather, the state of the economy or how nobody understands them. Being negative has become a habit and it is one that we need to ditch because, let's face it, who wants to listen to negativity morning, noon and night?

If we are positive and happy, good things will come our way. Try it for a week or so and see what happens. When you feel good, people want to be around you – they want some of what you have! There is nothing more attractive in this world than a happy, smiling man or woman, boy or girl. We all pick up on the energy that surrounds each one of us. If you arrive into school moaning about a test that you haven't studied for or giving out about a schoolmate because they are doing better than you, what type of energy are you giving out into the world? It is very hard to be around people who are constantly miserable because they make us feel awful too and why should you be responsible for anyone else's moods? It's not realistic to expect to be happy a hundred per cent of the time (heaven forbid), and we don't expect you to be insensitive to your friends when they are in trouble, but maybe we could all improve our lives significantly by practising gratitude every now and then.

How many of us remember to be grateful every morning when we wake up or just before we go to sleep for the night? We always get our children to list off three things that they are grateful for when we tuck them in for the night. Remember, focusing on the good brings more of the nice things into our lives. However, the reverse is also true. If life seems to be going wrong for you, no matter what you do, flip it over. Instead of focusing all of your attention on the disasters that seem to be following you around, find something, anything, even if it is only very small, and give thanks for it. Put all of your attention on that one little thing and observe how good you feel when thinking about it. Notice how much better you feel when you focus on pleasant and uplifting thoughts and ideas. Do yourself a favour and make this a daily habit and one which you will practise all of your life.

Why not make a gratitude box and leave it in your home? Put in slips of paper with funny, uplifting phrases and compliments and urge each member of your family to take one every morning before they go to school or work for the day. Try it and see how it works!

However, what happens if it's Monday morning in the depths of winter? The wind and the rain are howling outside your window pane. You wake up thinking that it is a Saturday, then you groan inwardly as the truth dawns and you think of the million and one things you have to do. You know that a gratitude box simply won't cut it. If this sounds like you, then try to remember that there are many, many girls your age in the world who do not have enough to eat, who do not have warm clothes, or a safe place to sleep. Some do not have parents to take care of them – perhaps it is already their responsibility to take care of their family. Many are struggling with serious health problems and do not have access to medicine or hospitals. Many live in parts of the world which are torn apart by war and have had to leave home to escape danger. Some are not receiving an education, as you are, and they are told that they should not dream of growing up to be a teacher or an engineer or an artist. They may not have many opportunities to hang out with their friends and just have fun.

Be thankful for what you have;
you'll end up having more. If you concentrate on what you
don't have, you will never, ever have enough.'
Oprah Winfrey

Now this is the essence of what we are discussing and the secret behind every successful and happy person out there. Think about your friends in or outside of school – do you have some who are always upbeat regardless of what is happening around them? Aren't they great fun to be around? Don't you leave their company feeling good about yourself and the world, as well as hopeful and energised? Do you want people to feel the same way about you? Well, practise gratitude and watch things changing for the better!

Let your attitude be one of gratitude.

So how do I practise gratitude?

Get a diary or a sheet of paper and write out in numerical order all the things you are grateful for **right now**. It is important that you focus on things that you enjoy doing at present – don't worry about things that you would like to accomplish in the future. Think about how you feel at this very moment and what makes you happy or grateful today and then off you go! When you have finished, you might wish to decorate your list to make it even more pleasing to the eye. Why not get some nice, colourful card and write on it? You could add photos or pictures from magazines to make it more personal to you. When you are happy with the end result, put your gratitude list in a prominent position in the house where you will see it at least once every day.

(S): I have my gratitude list on the wall right in front of my bed at home so it is the first thing I see every morning when I get out of bed, ready to face a brand new day. No matter how cold, dark and miserable it is outside, I always feel better when I glance at it because it serves to remind me how lucky I am.

Here are some of the things that our students wrote about – maybe they are things that you are grateful for also. If so, add them to your list!

Helpful people – 'I am so grateful for all the kind and wonderful people who help me every day.'

My bed – 'I love getting into my warm, cosy bed on a stormy winter's night, especially when my mum has put clean sheets on the bed.'

Enthusiasm – 'Life is simply too short to sit around being bored. Get out there and live it!'

Life – 'It is fantastic that we are actually here in this world. Living.'

Family – 'They are my foundation. A true gift.'

Friends – 'There is simply no way that I could survive without them.'

Love – 'This is the most important thing of all. It is truly amazing.'

Words – 'I would not be me without them.'

Acceptance – 'I am so grateful to those who accept me just as I am.'

Choice – 'I can choose to be happy every day.'

Music – 'It is a powerful and an integral part of our lives. How would we live without it?'

Colour – 'I love the colours in the natural world.'

Art – 'Art brightens the world and my life.'

Health – 'I'm pretty healthy so I'm grateful for that.'

Stars – 'They remind me of the words of Napoleon Hill: "To be a star you must shine your own light, follow your own path and don't worry about the darkness for that is when the stars shine brightest."'

Positivity blogs – 'I love reading these on a regular basis. I am so grateful for all the work these people put in to raise our spirits.'

Holidays – 'I just love them (especially Christmas!).'

Sunshine – 'I love when the sun is shining – it helps us all to shine a little brighter.'

Books – 'I'm always so grateful for the words of another.'

Organisation – 'This might seem sooo boring but I'm glad that I'm organised.'

Encouragement – 'So many people support me in my life and I'm so blessed to have them.'

Accountability – 'I'm so glad that I know I can take charge of my own life.'

Change – 'It can be scary but still so important.'

Home – 'I am so grateful for it. I know that I can take it for granted.'

Comfort – 'Comfort food, comfy clothes, comfy couch. What's not to like?'

Passion – 'I love seeing someone who is passionate about what they do or love.'

Positivity – 'Changes the way we look at the world.'

Kindness – 'Even the smallest act of kindness can turn my day around.'

So there you have it. Hopefully the above statements will help you on your way to creating your very own gratitude list that is unique to you and you alone. Finally, remember: when life is difficult (and it certainly will be from time to time) think of all the good things in yours and hopefully they will make you feel a little better. Good luck!

Journaling

Journaling is using a diary or notebook to express your feelings and any experiences and thoughts that you may be having. Some students will write every day in their journals, others now and then. Artistic students will often draw instead of compose, which is fine too. Others may choose to express themselves through photos or magazine pictures and newspaper clippings. Journaling is a means whereby young people can express in words or images what often cannot be vocalised.

Keeping a journal can help you, over time, to see or view your life from a bigger, clearer perspective. It can be very therapeutic to get all of your thoughts down on a fresh, blank page. When we see our thoughts materialised onto a sheet of paper it can help us to understand ourselves and what is going on more clearly.

The beauty about keeping a journal is that you are the only one who gets to read it. You have no audience; therefore the rules that apply in the real world simply do not apply here. So, let rip – pour out what you really think about yourself and your dreams for the future (and not everybody else's dreams for you), how you feel about your appearance, your love life, your friends, relationships with parents and any difficulties. Keep your journal in a safe place. Tell your parents that it is strictly off-limits; they should respect that. Remember, the sky is the limit. You can say whatever you need to without anybody else judging you – or, worse, criticising you. Doing this can be very liberating as you get to realise how you really feel about your life. We would encourage any young adult to keep a journal, regardless of what is happening in their lives. Self-expression is always to be encouraged. Go for it – you might even find that you enjoy it!

> Journaling can make you aware of how wonderful tiny moments in your life can be, so the big stuff seems less scary.

Why keep a journal?

Journaling can be particularly helpful if you are finding that life is difficult. Maybe you are suffering from illness, or your parents are getting divorced or separated, or you have lost somebody close to you. All of these experiences are very confusing and are usually times when a range of varying emotions may rise to the surface. These strong feelings can add to your distress. We are talking here about all of the negative emotions: fear, anger, self-doubt, grief, rejection, betrayal and loss. These emotions, when they do surface in our lives, do not feel good and can throw us off balance. They can be very hard to process and often leave us feeling drained. You may not want to talk to anybody about how you feel, because you may be embarrassed to admit it, or maybe you simply do not have the words to express yourself adequately.

When you are writing, think of the blank page of the diary or journal as your best friend in the world, someone who **really is on your side** and who wants only the best for you. For many of you, it can be really difficult to express these feelings, especially the dark and terrifying ones, to people who may misunderstand you. Adults often try to 'fix' the problem or, worse still, tell you that everything is all right when, in your eyes, it clearly is not. It could be that the words are there but there may be nobody around to hear them. If that is the case, **the journal is there waiting and eager to listen**.

Where and when to journal

Obviously, you need to find a time and a place that suits you best to write. Your bedroom is probably the best place; after all, you will need some place quiet and private. Try to make sure that you will not be disturbed. You might like to have soft lighting and music on to help you feel relaxed. It is not necessary to journal every day but, like everything, the more you do this, the more skilled you will get at it. Try to spend between twenty and thirty minutes journaling at a time – any less and you really will not have the time to get down what you need to on paper. Give yourself permission to spend some time on yourself so that you can nurture your own private inner world.

How to write

✦   No rules apply. If you want to draw and doodle, go for it.

✦ Some prefer to put pen to paper and let whatever is in their mind come out without any editing whatsoever. This is called 'stream of consciousness' or 'free expression'. See if it works for you – put your pen on the blank page and do not lift it for two minutes. If what you have written seems like garbage, do not despair: there could actually be some gems of wisdom in among the rubbish. These gems could help you to gain valuable insight into your world.

✦ Write song lyrics or poems (if you are feeling very inspired). You will be amazed at just how much creativity can be unleashed when you feel that nobody else is watching.

The unexamined life is not worth living.'

Socrates

What do I do if I just don't know where to start?

Like with all writing, the most difficult thing is sometimes knowing how to start. Get yourself a lovely journal. Go out and splash some cash on one that looks absolutely beautiful and that makes you feel good every time you lay your eyes on it. Buy one that is really colourful and cheerful and bright – one that makes you smile inside when you see it.

Try using the following questions and prompts to get yourself started and to fire up your creative engines.

1. If you were to describe yourself to an alien from outer space, what would you say?

2. How do you think your friends and family would describe you?

3. Why do you think it is important for you to keep a journal? Remember, **only you** know the answer to this one.

4. What are your **strengths** or your good qualities?

5. List one thing that you have done in your life that you are **proud** of.

6. How do you feel about the way you look? **Imagine your body as a good friend.** Write a letter to your body thanking it for all it has done for you over the years.

7. What makes you afraid? What makes you **happy**?

8. Draw or cut out something that represents you. Say why it does.

9. Write about your **dreams** for the future. Try to imagine yourself at some future date, maybe fifteen years from now when you are in your thirties. What do you look like? Is your hair short or long? Where do you live? Dream big – is it in that fabulous glass beach house with stunning views over the wild Atlantic or can you see yourself in a lofty penthouse in Manhattan? What clothes are you wearing? Designer suit (I'm thinking Prada) or jeans and flip-flops? Why? Do you have a job? If so, what is it? Are you a best-selling author or a brilliant director who has already been nominated for an Oscar? Maybe you are working in a donkey sanctuary on the Aran Islands? Are you single or married to a man who stops traffic with his good looks? Do you have a family, a dog or a goldfish? Really try to imagine yourself as an adult and have fun doing it!

10. What was the **happiest moment of your life**? Why?

Hopefully, some of the above statements will help to get you started. Don't be surprised when you start writing if you find that you cannot get the words down fast enough. When this happens, it is fantastic. Our advice would be to just go with the flow and let it all out. Remember, this exercise is for you and you alone. Protect yourself and respect your privacy. You do not need to share every aspect of your life with the world around you. Finally, we really hope that you enjoy getting to know yourself better. Happy scribbling!

Mindfulness

Mindfulness is the act of living in the now. It sounds unbelievably simple but, as 80 per cent of the time we are either worrying about the future or fretting about the past, it takes time and patience. But stick with it – this really works.

So what is it?

Mindfulness is all about just noticing your breath and accepting how you feel while keeping your mind on your breathing. The trick here is not to become overly concerned with whether you are breathing smoothly and evenly (which is clearly good) or whether you are taking short, shallow breaths (which can indicate a busier, more agitated state of mind). It sounds easy but you will be amazed at how many times your thoughts just wander off and where they will lead you. Try not to become too irritated with yourself when this happens. Just gently guide your mind back to your breath. Mindfulness can help us to take a step back and **observe** our thoughts and feelings without **reacting** to them. It is as if we are an objective observer, watching our thoughts playing out like an old movie on a screen. This is a valuable life skill and can result in you feeling less exhausted by life and more grounded. Over time, and with patience, you will lose the desire to control or change your emotions, which constantly come and go anyway. It can teach you to become more compassionate towards yourself too, because the truth is, the more willing you are to give yourself a break, the more you will come to realise that how you are feeling is just how you are feeling **at that moment**.

Right here, right now, that's how.

If you decide to do a course in mindfulness you will be introduced to Mindful Movement, the Body Scan and the Loving Kindness Meditation among others. While these are all fantastic ways of de-stressing and removing ourselves from our frantic lives, they can take up to forty-five minutes to complete. Many teenagers who lead active, busy lives might be put off by that time investment. So, before you resist, I have some good news. You can become mindful by taking any number of the following simple steps, which can be done just about anywhere and at any time.

Autopilot

Think of something that you do each and every day while 'zoning out'. These activities could include having a shower, brushing your teeth, getting dressed, travelling to school or even walking from class to class.

Once you have picked an activity – for example, brushing your teeth – do it while being **completely mindful**. You might like to notice how the brush feels in your hand, smell the toothpaste as you squeeze it onto your brush and then feel the brush moving up and down in your mouth, against your gums and your teeth. If you find your mind wandering (and chances are that you will) do not scold yourself. Just gently bring your attention back to the activity in hand. Try to be more mindful when you are out for a walk or jog in the beautiful countryside. Try to notice what you see, what you can hear, what you can smell. Doing this makes the exercise more meaningful and enjoyable.

Something we often do mindlessly is eating. Have you ever just wolfed a sandwich down on the run and had no idea what it tasted like? An exercise to practise every now and then is to eat a meal or drink a cup of coffee or tea mindfully. Really take the time to look at the food and beverage before you start. What can you see and smell at this stage? When you take your first bite or sip that first mouthful, really savour the flavour or aromas. Chew slowly and methodically. Feel the food in your mouth and notice the pleasure that can be derived from simple things. Really enjoy the act of eating and drinking. **Pay attention.**

What about practising mindfulness when you are stuck in a queue in the supermarket or at the shopping centre? Instead of getting angry about how slow the cashier is, or wondering why the woman in front of you is taking so long, use this 'empty time' to become more mindful. Breathe in and out and try to block out the noise around you. Ask yourself how you are feeling and try to remain detached when you discover the answer. What thoughts are centre stage? Label them 'thoughts' and then go back to focusing on the breath. **Remember, thoughts and feelings come and go.** By observing them in a neutral way, you are taking control of them rather than the other way around.

> All I have is this moment, so I owe it to myself to be present in it.

How long is long enough?

If you like the sound of all of this and you think that it might be something that you would like to try, it is recommended that you are consistent in your practice. Anything from three to thirty minutes, six days a week will do. If that sounds like a large chunk of time to take out of your busy schedule, begin slowly with baby steps. Even three minutes a day is a great start to really changing your life and taking control. The key here is to be patient and kind with yourself as you chart your progress. **Remember, we only have one life. We might as well be involved in it.**

So many of us are afraid to sit still with ourselves and observe what is happening each day. We busy ourselves at school, at work, at home and at the weekends. **It is as if *doing* has obliterated *being*.** The truth is, however, that all of us need to cultivate the art of being still. This practice will, in turn, help us to manage our busier times in a more productive way. Due to no fault of our own, we make our family and friends our number one priority. We become completely focused on their lives and their stories. Mindfulness encourages us to turn this attention, love and compassion inwards.

Why should teenagers practise mindfulness?

Mindfulness is now widely considered to be a very useful tool when it comes to dealing with stress, anxiety and depression. It can also help teens to be more productive when it comes to concentrating and studying and performing better in exams. In our school in 2015, the senior students were introduced to a six-week mindfulness course. Every Monday and Tuesday, they practised mindfulness for fifteen-minute sessions. We asked some of them to tell us what they thought of the sessions and urged them to be as honest as possible. Our questions and some of the students' response are below.

What does mindfulness mean to you?

✦ 'Mindfulness is about concentrating on the here and now. **It's about becoming more aware.**'

✦ 'It's about **taking the time to be still** and focus your attention on your body and inner-self. It empties your head and allows you to relax.'

✦ 'It's about taking time out to notice things that go on around you and within you.'

✦ 'Mindfulness is concentrating on the here and now and not **worrying about the future or past.**'

✦ 'It's about being in the moment, **centring yourself.**'

✦ 'It's about becoming aware of your body and **getting away from that voice that is constantly nagging us**.'

Did you enjoy it?

✦ 'Yes, it was nice to learn to use mindfulness correctly. Being honest, I haven't felt the need to use it, but I like knowing that I **can** use it.'

✦ 'Yes. I really enjoyed it and now I practise it three times a week for fifteen minutes.'

✦ 'I enjoyed some exercises and I do use it now to relax myself in stressful times.'

✦ 'I felt very relaxed and I enjoyed it; however, fifteen minutes wasn't long enough to fit everything in.'

✦ 'Yes! I learned to control my thoughts more and also to think before I react.'

- 'This helps you to stay calm and in control. It helps to prevent anxiety about exams from taking over. I sometimes practise mindfulness before I sleep to help me wind down!'

- 'I found it really beneficial and continue to practise it in my spare time.'

Should teenagers practise mindfulness? If yes, why?

- 'I think that mindfulness is important for teenagers as it teaches us to **focus on the present** as this is all we can control right now.'

- 'Yes, I find that it's **good for sleep, concentration, de-stressing and study.**'

- 'Yes, if they have time!'

- 'Yes, but I think that it needs to be guided. Doing it myself is less effective, worries get on top of my mind.'

- 'Yes. It helps you to slow down and relax and **eases your mind** for a period of time.'

- 'It helps with stress and concentration.'

- 'Yes!'

- 'It helps you to relax and sleep at night.'

> Mindfulness helps me to observe life rather than react to it.

The loving kindness meditation

This is a lovely practice for relaxing and taking stock and it always brings a pleasant feeling of inner peace. So, sit back in a comfortable chair or lie on a sofa or bed. Make sure that you are warm, but not too warm; otherwise you will find yourself falling asleep. Turn off the phone and ask your loved ones not to disturb you. Then, breathe deeply three times and repeat the following phrases in your mind as you do so: 'May I be well, may I be happy, may I be at peace.'

Or, if that doesn't appeal to you, try these or any other sentences that work for you: 'May I be filled with loving kindness, may I be healthy and safe, may I be truly happy and free!'

Don't worry if you feel foolish at first. So many of us find it hard to be kind and patient with ourselves. After a while, you will begin to view yourself in a much more loving way. This is really useful if you are having unpleasant or unsettling thoughts. **Loving yourself should be your number one priority at all times.**

The body scan

To start off, sit in a place that is quiet and warm. Try to ensure that no one will disturb you for the next forty minutes or so – don't be afraid to tell your family that you need this time alone to meditate. You never know – they might see how positively it is affecting your life and follow in your footsteps!

Sit in a chair or lie on a mat, bed or sofa. Make sure that you don't get so comfortable that you fall asleep. Wear loose, comfortable clothes that will not confine or restrict you in any way. Use a pillow for comfort if you want and a light blanket to keep you warm.

Close your eyes, place your arms by your side and get ready to spend some time on yourself. **Try to view this as a practice which will improve both your physical and mental health.**

There is no objective; all you have to do is **observe your breath from moment to moment**. Try to let go of the urge to control everything: this exercise is about letting everything go – well, at least for forty minutes. Let yourself be exactly the way you are right now: don't try to change anything.

There is no right or wrong way to do this meditation. Your mind may wander many times during the session. When you notice this, don't be hard on yourself; simply bring your attention back to your breathing.

It is also possible that you may find yourself drifting off to sleep as you do the body scan. Again, as before, don't berate yourself. Instead, why not be compassionate to yourself and re-focus on the breath and your breathing?

Observe your body as it is lying down right now. How does it feel at this moment? Are there any parts of your body that feel uncomfortable or painful? If so, just acknowledge them. Can you feel the floor as you lie on it or the back of the chair where you are sitting? Can you feel your entire body from head to toe?

So, let's start …

✳ Concentrate on your breath. Don't try to alter it in any way — just be with yourself moment by moment. Try to distinguish where you feel the breath most. Is it in your chest or your stomach? If you can, try to get a sense of your abdomen expanding with the in-breath and contracting with the out-breath. As you breathe out just let everything go and notice how your body is getting heavier and heavier …

✳ Now, focus your attention on the toes of the left foot: how do they feel, are they throbbing or even itchy? It is quite possible that you feel nothing at all. Do they feel hot or cold? Take each toe on your left foot and pay attention to how they feel.

✳ After this, move your attention to the bottom of the left foot. Notice the heel and the base of the foot. Focus on any sensations that you might feel at this very moment. Can you feel your foot touching against the floor or the blanket?

✳ When you are finished, move your concentration to the skin on the top of the left foot … go deep into the foot.

✳ Move your focus up to the left ankle, the inside, the outside and, again, deep into the ankle. Simply accept what is.

✳ When you have finished, gently move your focus to the lower leg, the shin bone and the calf muscles. Observe any feelings that you may have here. Maybe you feel aches and pains?

✳ Move your concentration to your left knee, and be aware of any sensations that might be there. Place your attention on the kneecap at the front, the back of the knee and the sides.

✳ Next, move up to the thigh: what sensations are there right now? Do you feel any discomfort? Does it feel numb or heavy? Do you feel anything at all?

✳ Bring your attention back to the breath and focus on the belly, rising and falling.

✳ Now move your attention to the toes on the right foot … Follow the same instructions as before and bring your attention from the toes to the top of the foot, the shin, the knee and the thigh.

✳ When you have finished, gently move your attention to your spine. Become aware of its expanse and the way it moves all the way up the back.

✳ Then, take in all of your upper back. Pay close attention to your shoulders as this is an area which often feels tense. If you notice that you are carrying a lot of stress in your shoulders, just be aware of this; do not judge yourself in any way. Just observe what is happening.

✳ As you move through the body, you may find that your mind is very busy. You could find yourself thinking about an upcoming exam or event or you may find yourself thinking about something that happened to you in the past. If so, don't worry, simply bring your attention back to the breath when you realise what has happened. This is very normal.

✳ Every time you do the body scan, you may find that you have a different experience. Some days you may be pleased with yourself for being mindful; others, you may find that your mind is like an over-excited puppy, racing from one thought to the next. That is fine – it's just life. You don't need to change a single thing: simply lie down on the floor and give yourself the gift of time.

✳ Move your focus now to your belly button, your stomach, the area just under the rib cage.

✳ Become aware of the chest area – see how your breath enters and exits your lungs. Notice your rib cage rising and falling with each breath.

✳ Focus now on your heart. Can you give it any love and compassion?

✳ Move up the body to the collar bone … are there any feelings or sensations here?

✳ When you are done, take in the entire front section of your body as a whole. Notice how each part is connected to the next.

✳ Move your attention down the body to the fingers: spend a few moments with each finger.

✳ Now, focus on the entirety of the hands, the palms and the back of the hands. Go deep inside …

✳ Move from the wrist to the elbow, noticing how each part feels. You could easily have different feelings in each arm – how does that feel?

✳ Spend some time observing your elbow … just watch without reacting.

✳ Move up to the top of the arms … be aware of the bones and the muscles.

✳ Next, travel up to your neck … the inside and outside of the neck. Can you feel the material of your top against your skin? Maybe you can feel the pillow or cushion you are lying on? If so, what does that feel like?

✳ Move up to your face, the jaw bone, the chin. Again, just bring your attention to this part of your body.

✳ Now, move your focus up to your mouth. Does it feel soft or dry, tight or slack? Focus on the inside, the teeth and gums.

✳ Move your awareness to the nose. Can you feel the breath coming in and out? What do you notice?

✳ What about your cheeks, your ears? Can you feel inside your ears?

✳ Move to your temples, eyes and eyelashes … Pay attention, what can you feel?

✳ How does your forehead feel? Is it tense?

✳ Get a sense of your whole face, your scalp, the back of your head – what is it leaning on? Can you feel the air around it?

✳ What about inside your skull? How does that feel?

✳ Finally, take a few deep breaths and feel them moving through all the areas of the body that you have just focused on. Breathe in and out, in and out.

Congrats for successfully completing your first body scan!

All of the above simple steps work to help us become a player in our own lives. You need to be patient with yourself.

If we want to become more mindful, a good idea, lastly, is to imagine a bubble of love and patience surrounding ourselves. The desire to control everything gradually recedes into the background and we will become less stressed as a result. Mindfulness gives us the option of making things better now.

Good luck!

Positive Affirmations

Every thought we think, every word and all our inner dialogues are affirmations. They are a reflection of our inner truth and what we perceive to be true. **Our beliefs are thought patterns that we have developed since we were born** and, generally, they work very well for us. However, it is possible that some of our negative beliefs may be working against us and might even be inappropriate. Positive affirmations are intended to challenge those negative beliefs, as they allow us to stop the flow of negative thoughts and words. Affirmations are not just about repeating words. The more aware you are of positively affirming yourself in your own words and thoughts on a daily basis, the quicker they will work for you.

What you tell yourself every day will either lift you up or tear you down.

Affirmations can help you to focus on what you desire. In fact, they can influence your entire sense of self. We often tell ourselves horrible and downright false things such as 'I'm useless' or 'I look ridiculous' or 'I'm so stupid' or 'I'm such an idiot'. Taking a second to say 'Wait a minute, I am not useless', 'I look pretty good' and 'I'm very artistic' will actually bring you to a state of feeling in control of your own thoughts.

Everyone has a constellation of qualities that makes them uniquely wonderful. Our 'imperfections' make us attractive — every freckle, every birthmark, every scar, every dimple and every beauty spot contributes to our uniqueness. Even when we doubt our own beauty, thankfully there are people around us who can clearly see and appreciate it and bolster our flagging self-esteem.

(S): One of my students was very down and I was constantly researching new techniques and exercises that I could use to help her. Affirmations worked really well for her. I urged her to repeat and really believe her chosen statement while looking in the mirror. Yes, she felt daft at first; however, I asked her to bear in mind that some of the most important messages we have all received have been from people looking us directly in the eye – it is important that we do the same. Doing this helps to magnify the importance of the message.

For some people, affirmations become much more effective when they are action-oriented. For example, saying 'Every day I am getting healthier and healthier' is an affirmation. However, you make it an action-oriented affirmation by saying something like 'Every day I am getting healthier and healthier by eating well and exercising.'

Writing your affirmations down is another powerful way of keeping them at the forefront of your mind. Leaving affirmation cards lying around the house or sticking them up so that you pay attention to them at various stages throughout the day can really help to raise your mood and put a pep in your step!

Here are some sample affirmations you may like to use:

✦ 'I like myself today. I know there are parts of me that I want to improve, but I don't want to be anyone else. I'm happy to be me.'

✦ 'I cannot see the outcome of my journey, but I am willing to take the next step.'

✦ 'I am healthy.'

✦ 'I am good enough just as I am.'

✦ 'I breathe in calmness and breathe out anxiety and stress. I am at peace.'

✦ 'Right now, I may not see the good in this situation, but it is there.'

✦ 'I am going to find optimistic and hopeful ways to look at this problem.'

✦ 'I love my family even if they do not completely understand me.'

✦ 'I choose friends who appreciate and love me.'

✦ 'Today I am happy to be alive, I am full of joy.'

- ◆ 'I deserve love and respect.'
- ◆ 'I am loved and love others.'
- ◆ 'Today I choose joy.'
- ◆ 'Today has limitless possibilities.'
- ◆ 'I can start healthy habits.'
- ◆ 'When I get stuck, I am patient and kind to myself.'
- ◆ 'I choose kindness; I will not be hard on myself today.'
- ◆ 'The more love I give, the more that love is returned to me.'
- ◆ 'I am not afraid of making mistakes.'
- ◆ 'I can go anywhere I want to go, one step at a time.'

Having a positive mind-set is a wonderful life strategy. Affirmations can help us to develop a powerful attitude to life which is like an energy source for success. Imagine starting your day by waking up every morning with a positive affirmation. Try it, it's worth a shot!

Relaxation

We live in a busy, chaotic world where people rush around, deadlines have to be met, exams studied for and things have to get done. It is almost like a badge of honour to admit to the world how busy our lives are. It is as if being busy equates with being successful. I think most of us know that this philosophy is slightly ridiculous, yet how many of us find it difficult to simply step off the treadmill and breathe?

We often spend time in the classroom urging students to slow down and relax. This may sound unorthodox but teenagers are prone to getting very stressed, especially when exams are looming. They seem to think that it is necessary to constantly study and work towards exams and exclude any form of relaxation whatsoever from their lives. We are constantly telling them to work hard during the week when they are at school, but to take some time out to recharge the batteries at the weekends. Often, we get horrified reactions, with teens saying 'But, I don't have the time to relax' or 'Tell that to my parents, they never let me go out. They expect me to study around the clock.' You need time away from your books and the pressures of school to be yourself and have some fun. You are more than just a grade. After all, if you are happy, you will perform better at school. Always.

Do one thing every day that you like. This could be anything: going for a quick run, watching your favourite soap on TV, listening to music or meeting friends for a chat over coffee. It simply doesn't matter what you choose to do – what is important is that you are giving yourself the gift of time, to do something which will brighten your day and make the world seem like a nicer place.

When I relax, my mind answers all my questions.

Never underestimate the power of fun

Remember, it is important to always give yourself time for enjoyment. Ask yourself – am I having fun in my life? And if not, why not? Enlist your friends;

they probably need a fun-injection too, especially if they're facing important exams or events in their lives. Why not take control and plan a night out? It is so important to have things to look forward to. Ask yourself: Is my life balanced at the moment or am I spending too much time studying? If so, can you allow yourself some time for you? Is it time to discover new things? There are so many different ways to enjoy yourself. Maybe you need to join a club or take up a new hobby. Is there something which you have always wanted to do but have consistently put off for a later date? Why not do it now?

Try to remember when you were a child. What did you love to do then to relax and pass the time? Children are amazing at how they can focus for a long time on a game or a story. Try to think back to when you were little and life was fun and you were always relaxed. Maybe you need to reconnect with your inner child and go for a bike ride with your kid brother or make a batch of cookies that you loved to devour when you were younger.

Learning to relax is a life skill, one which we think should be taught in schools around the globe. But how can you find out which relaxation technique is the one for you? We have already mentioned the power of being in the now and mindful breathing in our mindfulness chapter but what else can you do to help you cope with life and manage events and people in a way that is both easy and beneficial?

Exercise

Everybody knows that the benefits of exercise are enormous and far-reaching. It's simple: when you exercise, you feel good. That's why so many doctors recommend that patients suffering from depression get out in the open air and move about. Whenever life is getting on top of you and you are feeling stressed about schoolwork, people or situations, put on your running shoes and mentally push yourself out the door. Often, when feeling overwhelmed, the last thing you feel like doing is braving the elements and exerting yourself, but when you come back home sweaty, breathless and happy, you know in your heart of hearts that you did what you needed to do.

Of course, you don't have to run, but why not try some other form of physical exercise? You could go for a walk, join a swimming club or enlist in a team sport. We all know that Europe, and especially Ireland, is teetering on the verge of an obesity epidemic. Why not do yourself a massive favour and decide to get fit today? Your body and heart will thank you for it. Not only that, but you will be a much more relaxed person – what's not to like about that?

Because of the vital and often complex link between the mind and the body, when you relax your body, you relax your mind. So, if exam preparation is getting you down, do yourself a favour – give yourself a break for thirty or forty minutes a day and get out into the fresh air. Look around you, take in the beauty of our wonderful planet and smile. Add some physical exercise to this and you have a very potent and powerful combination indeed.

A quick-fix relaxation meditation

As always, wear loose clothing and sit or lie (if you are sure you won't fall asleep) in a comfortable position. Make sure that you are warm and turn off your phone and try to make sure that you won't be disturbed for ten minutes.

1. Close your eyes and roll your eyeballs up in their sockets slightly. This is the position they are in when you are asleep. Doing this can help trick the brain into thinking that it is now time to relax.

2. Breathe in through your nose and out through your mouth. Be aware of the weight of your body on the chair, sofa, mat or bed. Feel your whole body getting heavier and heavier. If you have any aches or pains, focus your attention on them as you continue to breathe in and out.

3. After a few minutes of this deep, relaxing breathing, picture clearly in your mind's eye a time in your past when you felt super relaxed. Imagine this place, paying attention to as many details as you can. If you can't think of a time, invent a special place in your mind. It could simply be your bedroom at home or someplace else where you felt safe.

4. Begin to say to yourself, 'I am relaxing, I am relaxing, I am becoming more and more relaxed.' Bit by bit, and with practice and patience, you will feel your body beginning to loosen up as you go deeper and deeper into relaxation. When you focus on your ideal place, you will also notice that your mind begins to slow down. After a number of minutes, you will feel pleasantly relaxed and at ease.

5. After about ten minutes, five if you have just begun the process, open your eyes and bring yourself slowly back into the room. Notice how much better you feel. Remember, you can re-enter this private and safe space whenever you wish. All you have to do is allow yourself some 'me time'.

Self-massage

Massage is another effective form of relaxation. Neck and shoulder tension can be an issue for students, which is hardly surprising considering the heavy bags that you carry. Also, you often spend large parts of your day sitting in bad work positions. A massage from a professional therapist can be an incredible way to help your body feel refreshed, but self-massage is effective too. With self-massage you can ease the pain; the solution is literally at your fingertips.

It is no surprise that the popularity of massage is soaring, given the many benefits it has for body and mind. It can alleviate tension from muscles that have tightened due to stress. It is also important to always stretch the muscles out after massaging the area. If you are in pain, you should never use self-massage as a substitute for proper medical treatment. Applying heat to your neck, followed by gentle stretching, will help to decrease tension in the neck and shoulder muscles. Generally, you can stretch these muscles by tipping your head to the side, bringing your ear towards your shoulder. Hold the stretches for twenty to thirty seconds and repeat two or three times.

While sitting at your study area, rest your elbows on your desk and allow your head to drop slightly forward. Use your fingertips or thumbs, whatever feels most comfortable to you. Apply small strokes in either a circular motion or back and forth to massage your neck from your shoulders to the base of your skull. Ensure that the movements are strong enough so that it feels good, but not so hard that it hurts. Then interlace your fingers and place your hands on the back of your head. Drop your head forward and tuck your chin in towards your chest, applying gentle pressure to the back of your head. This stretches the muscles of your neck and those that run down along your back.

Yoga or stretching

In our school, fourth years have a yoga module which they follow for a period of six weeks. Nearly always, the students say how fantastic the classes are and how relaxed they feel afterwards. If this appeals to you and you feel that yoga might be something that you would enjoy, why not check out the times and venues where classes are being held in your local area? Over the last decade, yoga has become extremely popular and there are people of all ages enjoying classes on a weekly basis up and down the country.

What is yoga?

Yoga has been defined as a spiritual, physical and mental discipline that aims to transform body and mind (Wikipedia). It is practised all over the world for health and relaxation. In our crazy world, we have become used to looking outside of ourselves for happiness and a sense of self-worth. We are told again and again that possessions and material goods can make us happy. However, most of us know that this is a lie. It is as if we are always looking for peace, relaxation, contentment and, yes, happiness in the world around us. Often, no matter how successful we become, there still seems to be something missing. It is as if happiness is always just out of reach …

The truth is, of course, that true happiness lies within and that is where yoga comes in. Yoga helps us to realise that being is more important than doing. There is a saying in the Bible: 'Be still and know that I am God.' Yoga helps us to still our sometimes frantic and chaotic minds and, like mindfulness, is another invaluable tool in helping teens and people of all ages to relax. When we still our thoughts we begin to see who we really are. Still interested? Well then, find a class close to you. Or why not be proactive and assertive and ask your school to run one for the students?

If yoga sounds too time-consuming and expensive, why not engage in some cheap and simple morning stretches?

Five-minute morning stretching programme

1. Sit on the floor with your legs out in front of you. Focus on your breathing. Keep your attention on the breath as you carry out the session.

2. Move your shoulders up and down freely. After this, slowly move your arms around in a clockwise direction.

3. Interlock the fingers of both hands and stretch them above your head, taking care to clasp your hands throughout.

4. After this, move your head around slowly in an anticlockwise direction. Then clockwise. Then simply move your head up and down slowly, taking care to stretch out your neck where a lot of tension can be held.

5. Sit back down on the floor. Stretch out your legs in front of you. Lean forward, placing your hands on the tops of your feet, and breathe. This is a very effective exercise for stretching out your back.

6. Lastly, stand tall, breathing in and out deeply for ten breaths. You are now ready to face your day!

To conclude: remember, we all feel stressed from time to time. We wouldn't be human otherwise. What is important, though, is to make time in our daily lives for some fun and relaxation – at least thirty minutes a day. It is up to you to find something that will help you to lead a more relaxed and therefore productive life.

It's your life – enjoy it!

Creative Colouring
and Mandalas

In the middle of our hectic lives, fraught with deadlines and social pressure, we are bombarded with a sensory overload of information on a daily basis. Sometimes it's essential to take time out, to find peace and quiet and have moments of self-reflection. Mandala colouring is an effective way to help quieten the mind from the rush of constant chatter and can establish a sense of inner calm. Focusing on colouring or designing a mandala can help to bring balance and harmony into your life. It can also alleviate anxiety and facilitate a movement into the 'now' and present, promoting mindfulness. Mandalas have been used by many ancient cultures as a symbol of wholeness. Carl Jung, a Swiss psychiatrist, believed that drawing mandalas was a healthy form of self-expression. He believed that the hands will often find the answer to problems the mind is wrestling with.

Designing your own mandala

Tibetan Buddhist monks choose to study the art of designing mandalas in order to attain mindfulness because they knew that all that we need lies within.

It is a useful meditative exercise and with some art materials and some quiet time you can design your very own mandala. The mandala is widely recognised as a geometric design intended to symbolise the universe. Usually constructed within a circle, it can be viewed as a container of your own inner symbols which arise during its creation. The origin is the centre, this is the starting point; begin by focusing your energy on this central point. Designing or colouring a mandala can have a therapeutic effect. It stimulates both the right and left side of the brain, our mind is taken off our worries and stress reduces.

What you will need

You will need a quiet space where you won't be interrupted. Some paper, pencils, markers, paint or crayons and a compass. Be as adventurous as you wish and remember there is no right or wrong way.

Take a few moments to relax, focus on your breath. Allow and welcome images to arise in your mind, be aware of colours, shapes, symbols, i.e. animals, flowers, swirls, waves, etc.

Using a compass or circular object, draw a circle. Starting at the central point, begin to doodle spontaneously, let your feelings and instincts guide you to choose colours and shapes until the circle is full; if possible try to balance the four quadrants of the circle.

Take a few moments to reflect on your mandala, being aware of any repeating patterns, rhythms or symbols. Does your mandala tell a story? Take a few moments to write them down and be aware of any emotions that may have come to the surface during the process. Keep your mandala in a safe place as it is your creation and a reflection of you.

We've included some examples on the next few pages to get you started.

Words of Wisdom to My Teenage Self

(M): If I could have any super power, it would definitely be the ability to time travel. I would love to be able to turn the clock back and have a little chat with my teenage self. I would probably tell her to trust herself more, to stop worrying about the future and perhaps to re-think the dodgy perm and the metallic blue space boots...

(S): I was the anxious girl with the bad haircut who never gave herself enough credit. I would tell my younger self that, yes, she will definitely make some impressive mistakes, but that these important life lessons are actually what will help her to grow and turn into the person she is meant to be. Learn from all your experiences. They are valuable. It is not just the peaks but also the valleys that help you to grow and develop. You can handle so much more than you give yourself credit for. Face the world head-on and never apologise to anyone for being yourself.

Stop waiting and start living. Life happens now!

Remember:

✸ You are always well-dressed when you are wearing a smile.

✸ Stop being so scared. Fear can hold you back and stop you from living. Affirm yourself.

✸ Be nice to yourself and be happy. You cannot put a price on happiness. One negative thought can quickly spiral into a thousand, so always try to find the positive in every situation.

'You must be the best judge of your own happiness.'

Jane Austen, 'Emma'

✳ **Be grateful for everything in your life.** Take time to be appreciative every day. You can open new doors with grateful thoughts. Say 'thank you' to people for everything they do. Appreciate others. Gratitude leads to happiness and success.

✳ Your faithful friends are a genuine treasure. **Appreciate your friendships.**

✳ Stay true to yourself and do not give in to peer pressure.

✳ Grades measure your performance in school, but your performance in life in general is measured by intelligence. Do not get stressed about exams. Find a balance in life between your schoolwork and extracurricular activities and your need for sleep and fun.

✳ You will experience loss in your life but **you will cope, you are stronger and bigger than you think**.

✳ Don't hold onto relationships that hurt – accept only what makes you feel great.

✳ Accept yourself just as you are and stop trying to live up to other people's expectations. **Stop seeking external validation.** The goal is not to stop reaching out to others. It is to be there for yourself first.

✳ Do not take on other people's issues. You have to remember that caring about someone and taking on their problems are **two very different things**. Taking on someone else's worries and problems doesn't help them or you; it just drains you of energy that you could be using to support them. You do not have to stop listening or being a supportive friend; you just have to stop holding others' problems within.

✳ Learn to be alone and enjoy your own company.

Being happy doesn't mean that everything is perfect.

- Stop worrying, wondering and doubting and just believe that things will work out, maybe not as you planned but how they are meant to be.
- Do not blame everything and everyone for your mistakes, frustrations and failures. Take responsibility – deal with it, learn from it and move on.
- Exercise: it releases endorphins, which make you happy.
- Try to remember that there are always two sides to **every** story. Do not jump to conclusions. Get the facts first, then make up your own mind.
- Think before you act.
- Everything happens for a reason. Constant smooth seas do not make skilful sailors.

'Trust that everything happens for a reason, even when you're not wise enough to see it.'

Oprah Winfrey

- Try to do one **random act of kindness** every day.
- Everyone feels lost sometimes. **Trust** that it is all going to work out for the best.
- Be inspired by others but **celebrate your uniqueness**. Be the best that you can be.
- Stop and think before judging others. Show empathy and try to put yourself in their shoes.
- Every day is a new beginning, **release the past**. Let go of anger and hurt – it only leads to unnecessary stress.

✳ Accept that everyone has different standards. Break free from your expectations and understand that other people's viewpoints and priorities may be different from yours. You have no control over how they think or operate.

✳ **Stop comparing yourself** to others. Accept yourself just as you are. **You are enough.**

✳ Nothing is insurmountable – every obstacle can be conquered.

✳ You can never please everyone. **Accept that not everyone will like you.**

✳ Stop being a perfectionist – you will be much happier when you learn to let things go. It is OK to make mistakes. So **worry less and have more fun**.

✳ Be open to receiving help from others as you navigate life's path.

✳ **Dream, Dream, Dream!**

'Every great dream begins with a dreamer.'

Harriet Tubman

Final Note

One of the most important reasons for embarking on this journey was that we wanted girls like you to look at yourself and realise just how fantastic you really are.

Again and again we see teenage girls trying to come to terms with adulthood and the world around them. So many self-help books have been written exclusively for parents about 'surviving the teenage years', yet as far as we can see, nobody seems to be writing for young people. Even though we firmly believe that you are the ones who really matter.

We would say to you that, no matter what is going on around you, there are two things that you can always control: your thoughts and your breath. Master these and you can move mountains and do absolutely anything! Life is not supposed to be so difficult – it is meant to be fun and exhilarating. If you do nothing else today, please remember that thoughts are only thoughts; they come and go all the time, sometimes at a break-neck and alarming speed. If you are prone to self-sabotage (and, let's face it, who isn't?) there is comfort in knowing this simple but powerful truth. You can decide what you want to think about, so why not make the decision to think nurturing and supportive thoughts about yourself?

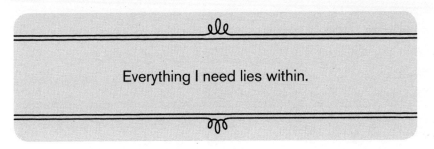

Everything I need lies within.

Even though you probably don't think about it very often (if at all), your body is constantly working hard to support your very existence by breathing in and breathing out for you all the time. No matter how stressful or difficult your day may be, put your hand on your stomach and breathe in and out deeply and calmly for a few minutes. Notice the subtle changes in your body; you will feel calm, connected and more content in a matter of seconds. Give it a try the next time you are feeling a bit overwhelmed – you will be pleasantly surprised at the difference this simple exercise makes to your sense of balance and well-being.

'What lies behind us and what lies before us are tiny matters compared to what lies within us.'

~ Ralph Waldo Emerson ~

Encouraging self-esteem is the key to your success in life. When you build on your self-esteem, your life will automatically become more enjoyable. You will believe in yourself and have the confidence to shine – you will be able to speak your mind and feel strong enough to make the right choices for you and you alone. Try not to bottle things up: it is much healthier to express how you really feel. Observe the way you talk to yourself and be very vigilant. Speak kind and empowering words to yourself today and watch how your life improves for the better.

There really is no point waiting around for some beautiful stranger to come and rescue you and sort all your problems in the blink of an eye – you can take control of your own life and your own destiny. Self-love can change your life – when you shine love on yourself and open up your heart, often you will notice that things will begin to (almost miraculously) fall into place and the world begins to make sense again. You have all that you need within you to live a fabulous and exciting life. Sometimes, you just have to be brave enough to look inwards and listen attentively to your heart.

Trust in yourself.

Believe that you can do anything you set your mind to and others will too. You are the expert at being you. So never allow other people to tell you how you should feel or what you should think. Don't be a doormat or a people pleaser – you will only end up in a state of disillusioned exhaustion and may even lose sight of who you really are. Do your actions scream to the world that everyone else's wishes are somehow more important than yours?

Maybe it is time to go out and reclaim your life, your happiness and your identity.

*Why should we worry about what others think of us,
do we have more confidence in their opinions
than we do our own?*

— Brigham Young —

We are not saying that your search for empowerment will always be an easy one. However, we believe that the best things are always worth fighting for. Of course, there will be bumps on the road ahead but try to remind yourself that if there weren't, life would be very dull indeed.

Dream big – don't take a back seat in your own life because, before you know it, you'll be celebrating your fiftieth birthday and wondering where the last thirty odd years have gone! Go out and grab your life firmly by the shoulders and remember: never be afraid.

For Parents: What Do Teens Want?

The teenage years can be a minefield for any unsuspecting parent out there. One minute, your daughter is an adoring eight-year-old who loves playing with her dolls and Lego and insists on having you read to her before she goes to sleep at night. Fast forward six or seven years, though, and the landscape has changed significantly. You find yourself in undiscovered territory and you don't know which way to turn. She has grown a few feet, is demanding that she get a tattoo and is hanging out with boys that you (we are talking to the dads here) don't trust because they remind you too much of what you were like at that age! For mums, it's no different. You are no longer the centre of her universe (her friends are) – instead you feel like public enemy number one. You have every right to feel unprepared, baffled and stressed. Perhaps you find that you are asking yourself over and over: 'What have I missed?' 'What has just happened?'… Know that you are not alone.

Our objective is to provide honest, practical advice which we hope will help you to navigate the sometimes stormy waters of adolescence and also guide your daughter through what has become an increasingly threatening society. By developing an open and nurturing relationship, you will help her to set aside her fears of not being good enough and, instead, allow her to be the best that she can be, so that she can shine from the inside out and make the world a better place.

We have always found teenagers to be completely honest. They will speak openly and frankly about their experiences if they feel that it is safe to do so and they won't be ridiculed in any way for their beliefs. One of the things that frustrates them most is when adults don't take their beliefs seriously – or, worse still, ignore them altogether. It is very important to give young girls a platform to speak; this can be difficult, especially when we don't like what they have to say.

Recently, we asked a group of senior students to talk about what they wanted from their parents. The one thing that kept being repeated by the girls was how much they loved their mums and dads. So that is the good news. However, many felt that their parents tried to present an idealised version of themselves as teenagers. And guess what? None of the students believed them. Many of the girls said how they wished that their parents could remember that they too were once teenagers dealing with the stresses and anxieties that adolescence brings. They said that if parents were open and honest and communicated freely about how they managed their adolescence, this would help and bring them closer rather than further apart. It is interesting that a lot of them said that they don't expect their parents to be perfect (thank God for that) but they would like if their parents tried to understand their world.

A question worth asking might be 'How can I be more of the parent that I wish I'd had?' As a young person, did you wish that your parents listened to you and cherished your emerging sense of self and trusted you to take your place confidently in the world? It would appear that this is what young people want most of all. They all want to be told that they are good enough.

We asked the girls what they would tell their parents if they were honest and brave enough. The following are some of their comments.

THINGS WE'D LIKE OUR PARENTS TO KNOW

Mum – don't worry about the weird clothes, music and boyfriends. I need to find out who I am – give me the space to do that.

I know that a lot of the time I act like I know it all. Truth is, I haven't got a clue. That's scary.

'All of my changing moods are confusing. One minute, I'm happy; the next, I'm angry. What's that about?'

'I sometimes miss how close we were when I was little. I don't always know how to bridge the gap between us.'

'It would really help if you pointed out all the things that I'm doing right, instead of constantly reminding me of all that I am doing wrong.'

'I don't want to be the adult in the house. That is your job.'

'You have to let me make mistakes. How else will I learn about life? I know that you want to protect me from everything, but that suffocates me. I need space to discover who I am.'

'I don't want you to be my friend; I have enough of those already. Just be my mum.'

'Please don't be awkward about my boyfriends. That makes me feel awkward too.'

'I still need to talk to you, but I don't know how to sometimes.'

'I get anxious when I see you stressed. I want you to take care of yourself.'

'You need to talk about the issues – the awkward stuff. If you don't, I think that either you can't be bothered or you don't know how.'

'Please, please, please – go out and have some fun. I can't handle being the centre of your universe.'

'Even though you'd never guess it in a million years, I love you to bits.'

So parents, take heart; even though your daughter seems grown up, sophisticated and worldly wise, she still needs you **more** than ever. She just may not be able to express it. If you both take the time to **really** listen to each other, this will ultimately enhance your relationship and bring you closer together. We wish you the best of luck.

Below are just a few of the topics we've been asked about over the years. We decided to discuss all the common issues that teenagers worry about. We want to offer positive tips and strategies and provide honest, practical advice which we hope will help.

1. Conflict resolution

'Before I got married I had six theories about raising children; now I have six children and no theories.'

John Wilmot

Nobody likes fighting. We all want to resolve conflict in a way that makes those involved feel that their needs are being met. Achieving this win–win solution, however, isn't always possible because we are only human.

> **(M):** Recently my nine-year-old daughter gave her father a Valentine card. In it she wrote, 'Dear Daddy. I love you with all my heart and think you are cool, funny and smart.' When I read

it, I decided there and then that I would frame the sentiments and show them to my husband in about six years' time when our daughter is slamming doors, sulking, going out with strange-looking individuals until all hours of the night and screaming at her dear old dad, telling him that he is the biggest loser she has ever met. Ever.

Parents – accept that you will make mistakes!

'Trust yourself. You know more than you think you do.'

✒ Benjamin Spock ✒

There are nights when you are tired and frustrated and yet you still have to prepare the dinner, feed the dog, make the lunches for the next day, phone your mother-in-law and do a million and one things before you collapse in an exhausted heap into bed. On days like these, the last thing you need is a stand-off with your teenage daughter. The truth is, of course, that we all lose our temper and say things that we don't mean. The aim is to control disagreements rather than let them control us. Frequent outbursts and abusive yelling can cause anxiety for everyone involved. When you are feeling deflated and wondering where your little princess has gone, remember Dory's words of wisdom in *Finding Nemo*: 'Just keep swimming, just keep swimming …'

Remember that you are both doing your best.

Parenting is not about perfection

Staying level-headed is important for health and sanity, as well as for our relationships. Remaining calm paves the way for more connected relationships. Your daughter is probably beginning to practise independent thinking, which is a necessary development but one which can lead to disagreements at home. Young people learn conflict management from watching what goes on around them, so try to be good role models and support, love and guide them along the way. Accept that, no matter how much you love each other, there **will** be moments when you may feel frustrated and completely out of your depth and this is fine. Parenting is not about perfection. Our job is to have the strength to work together with our children and do our best to solve conflicts in a respectful manner.

Teenagers need rules to guide and direct them in life. Too little discipline will lead to resentment but parenting that is too rigid is not beneficial either. The aim is to try to strike a balance between freedom and obedience, so that teenagers get a chance to develop problem-solving and leadership skills without feeling suffocated or restricted.

It is never too early to teach your daughter independence and the necessary skills to handle confrontation. If you constantly fight her battles, rescue her and smooth things over, you are preventing her from developing essential strategies to overcome difficulties in life. A key role in parenting is preparing your daughter for how the world really works.

Every day in the classroom, we apply many of these conflict resolution strategies with our students. There are times when we **all** need to turn inwards and see what we can change about our own attitude when dealing with difficult situations. Ask yourself are you commanding or cooperative? Do you really listen to your daughter's point of view?

TIPS FOR RESOLVING CONFLICT

- ✪ Teens and their parents should try to respond to and resolve issues in a positive manner, rather than being reactive and demanding the final say.

- ✪ Ensure that **all the family** plays a part in resolving conflict. Working together is much more effective than focusing on control. Discussing what you are all thinking and examining those choices can lead to more effective resolutions.

- **Open-ended questions** can lead to better communication, so rather than blaming and accusing each other, you could stop and ask:
  - 'Tell me why do you think that?'
  - 'What other feelings or thoughts do you have about this?'
  - 'How do you propose we achieve this?'
  - 'What do you think we should do?'

  By posing these questions your teen will feel **relaxed** and safe enough to express what she really thinks in front of you. Peaceful conflict resolution teaches teenagers about how to calmly and respectfully argue their point of view. Ask:
  - 'Can you please give me a valid reason to support why you feel your idea is so important?'
  - 'Please try and explain why this means so much to you.'
  - 'I don't think that is possible but can you think of other ways we could work this out?'

  Accept when their reasons are valid. Being flexible helps when you are frantically trying to find a compromise that works for everyone. Agreeing on a solution is a skill that becomes easier with practice.

- Calm down first. Don't be afraid to rewind and start over. Emotions can often prevent us from identifying the real problem. Say things like 'Arguing is not getting us anywhere. We need to talk. Why don't we take a few minutes to cool down, think and try again?' You could also say, 'I can see that you really want this and, rather than rush into a decision, let's process it and think it through.' Managing to remain serene allows us to see the bigger picture; it also helps us to realise that smaller issues are often the symptoms of a larger problem.

- Always try and put yourself in the other person's shoes. That way, you can understand the problem from their perspective.

- Set aside time every week to discuss issues or disagreements in a peaceful manner. This way, requests can be respectfully met and issues resolved before they escalate.

- Communicate **realistic expectations** to each other. Be sensitive. The inflection of your voice, body language, body movement and other non-verbal cues can affect communication.

✪ Listen to each other without interrupting or jumping to conclusions. Be willing to accept that you might not be right. Be able to apologise and forgive. When you get angry, you have gone beyond the argument. It now becomes about winning. Avoid this at all costs.

✪ There are times when parents have to say 'No'. Try to say it in a kind way, such as 'I know this is not what you want to hear, but it is my job to keep you safe and my final answer is no.' Be understanding and supportive. Let your daughter express and process her feelings.

✪ Things get said in the heat of the moment. Try not to take criticism or disagreements personally. It can be hard to channel feelings of unconditional love when your teenager is shouting at the top of her voice 'I hate you!' or 'You are ruining my life!' Really, they are just looking for attention in a hurtful way. Do not be drawn into confrontation.

✪ Constantly fighting is pointless. **Pick your battles.** If you are having a disagreement, do not throw the whole kitchen sink into the argument. Do not say, 'Last week you said this and a month ago you did that.' Prioritise and deal with the issue at hand.

✪ Sometimes, we need to stop and refocus. Ask yourself, 'What are we really fighting about?'

✪ When you feel angry, it is important to stop and breathe deeply. Deep breathing can help the irritation and rage to melt away. Some people like to have a list of positive things about their teen at hand which they can read at a time of conflict. They then feel like they can return to the issue and tackle the conflict in a more positive way.

✪ Try to be mindful. At times, we are so busy thinking about everything that needs to be done that we forget to focus on each other. When we do, positive solutions can be reached and miracles can appear. Good luck!

2. Friendships

As your daughter enters adolescence, friends become more important and can become one of the greatest influences in her life. You now play a very different role in your daughter's life, and often you might feel that you just don't matter any more. While you influence her long-term decisions, her friends influence decisions in the short term. You may feel frustrated at the amount of time she spends with her close friends; however, in order for your daughter to grow into a well-adjusted and balanced adult, it is important that her relationships both inside and outside of the home are strong. Get to know her friends and show her just how much you value her friendships too.

Most teenagers just want to belong. Your daughter is simply trying to find herself, gain independence and develop autonomy. Listening to the same music and dressing in the same way as friends are just ways of expressing herself. It can be helpful to compromise with your daughter – if wearing ripped jeans makes her feel connected to her peers, is it really necessary to fight with her?

Teenagers need their parents. The peer pressure they face on a daily basis (drinking, smoking, taking drugs, casual sex) can be a heavy burden on their shoulders and it may sometimes feel like it is impossible to deal with. However, having a supportive adult on their side can make all the difference.

Strategies for dealing with peer pressure

✵ Parents need to boost their daughters' confidence. Teenagers often feel that they need to conform in order to fit in with their peer group. However, the more confident a teenager is, the more successful they are at resisting negative peer pressure. Teach your teenager to stop, breathe, think and listen to her instincts.

✵ Role play situations with your teenager and suggest ways she can say 'No'. That way, she feels prepared when difficulty strikes. She is also less likely to be caught off-guard and end up doing something she does not want to do or something that she will later regret.

✵ Give your teenager a get-out clause. By doing so, you are, in essence, giving her a support system that she can use until she has developed a strong enough sense of herself. You are not fighting her battles for her but giving her a scaffold until she is strong enough to support herself. Tell her that she can ring you with a coded message, like checking in on a sick relative, and you will know that it means that she needs a hand.

✷ Remind your daughter that, at times, her friends may lie to appear 'cooler'. Tell her if she ends up copying them she could end up with a bad reputation or worse.

✷ Support your teenager. Encourage her to accept her 'perfect imperfections'. She will feel more confident in making her own decisions and resisting peer pressure if she has a strong sense of self-worth and self-belief.

✷ Encourage your daughter to have her friends around. Make them feel welcome in your home. That way, you are more aware of any negative peer pressure that is becoming an issue. Build a positive relationship with your daughter so that she feels that she can rely on you. Try to encourage your daughter to pick a sensible and smart group of friends. Peers who have a good outlook and attitude will not force or encourage her to do 'risky' things.

✷ Your teenager is watching you **all** the time. She notices the way you handle situations and make difficult decisions. Teach her how you resolve uncomfortable predicaments in a positive way.

✷ Encourage your daughter to think for herself. Show her how to make simple decisions, so that when tough decisions have to be made, she will be able to choose right from wrong.

✷ Be involved in her life and pay close attention to her. When you are involved in her world you will notice changes in sleep and eating habits. Be ready to step up to the mark when she really needs you.

✷ Don't preach. If she can see that you can listen more than preach, she'll be sure to touch base with you if she really needs to talk.

✷ Self-confidence affirmations repeated over and over **can** help build her confidence. For dealing with peer pressure, a good affirmation is 'I courageously face difficult situations with conviction and always find a good solution.'

Parents, you will come across uncomfortable situations where you must stand firm and be the parent. It is not always easy to lay down the law, but if you feel that toxic friendships are negatively influencing your daughter, you must stand firm and stick to the house rules. It can difficult, but your children need, and will hopefully come to respect, the boundaries you set for them. Ultimately this will teach them to establish important boundaries for themselves.

'Tell me and I forget, teach me and I may remember, involve me and I learn.'

~ Benjamin Franklin ~

Raise your teenagers to be confident and courageous. Despite what they say or do, let them always feel accepted, supported and loved.

3. Relationships

How do I help my teen through heartache?

Adults often view teenage relationships as puppy love, but when a relationship ends, it can be devastating. Your child has lost someone special in her life – she needs to be reassured that she is loved and lovable and that accepting, appreciating and loving herself is ultimately the path to finding her dream relationship. Her break-up can feel like a tsunami of shock, disbelief, denial and confusion, as waves of torrential sadness wash over her. In the early stages, it can appear overwhelming and unbearable for her and everyone in the family. It's quite possible that you just don't know what to do. However, in time she will find the resilience to survive and rebuild her world.

When we see our children hurting we instinctively want to take their pain away. Saying things such as 'they were never right for you anyway' or 'you deserve someone much better' are the clichéd lines teens say they hate hearing. Showing empathy by saying things like 'I'm so sorry you have to go through this pain' or 'I know it really hurts to lose someone you love' provides an opportunity to open up honest and helpful conversations.

Give your daughter as much space as she needs. Don't force her to talk. You can't take her pain away but when she wants to speak to you let it happen naturally. Just be there and listen so that she knows she has your support. If your child talks to you, give her your undivided attention. Let her vent so she has an outlet for her thoughts. Provide non-judgemental surroundings. If she is unable to find a safe environment to work through her pain, she may find unhealthy ways to deal with it. She may not confide in you, but it is important that your daughter can talk it out with someone who can support her.

Encourage her to stay busy as it will take her mind off the break-up and constantly remind her of her value. Suggest that she takes time out from technology. Rushing to Facebook to update her status or bad-mouth her ex is never a good idea. She needs time to process the hurt and allow it to heal. Everyone experiences heartache and comes out the other side wiser. Ultimately remind yourself that break-ups help us to grow stronger. Allow her to learn from the experience. Give her time – with support your daughter will emerge more resilient in the face of challenges.

Parent–teen relationship

For some parents, the teenage years can feel like a resurgence of the 'terrible twos', complete with the search for independence and the frustration at being unable to express the intricacies of their emotions. In order to preserve parent–teen relationships, and everyone's sanity, it is important to pick your battles. You may not be able to walk in your teenager's shoes, but you do need to try to understand and relate to her. Keeping the lines of communication open, providing support and listening to your teenager's concerns is necessary when it comes to surviving the teenage years. Supporting your daughter does not necessarily mean agreeing to her every request. Remember – you are still responsible for setting appropriate limits.

We often find it hard to relate to the hormonal and emotional changes teenagers are going through. The phrase 'You just don't understand me' has been heard by every parent at some stage. Although parents have lived through puberty and experienced their own emotional issues, they are probably no longer able to fully understand the mind-set of a teenager. At this stage of their lives, teenagers are **trying to distinguish themselves from their parents**, which is an important step in creating a healthy identity.

Parents have a profound impact on their daughters' lives. As she continues to grow and deals with issues that can be fraught with complications, parents should continue to work on building a trusting relationship and showing affection as she discovers more about who she is and what kind of person she wants to become.

Your involvement in your daughter's life is a crucial ingredient in her development as a young woman. By taking the time to encourage her, listen to her thoughts and build on her self-image you will reduce her insecurities and increase her confidence in her abilities.

Attempts to converse with your teen may be met with negative reactions, slamming doors or monosyllabic grunts. Remain calm … Do not give up … Persevere … It takes time and effort but eventually your daughter will open up. It is important that your daughter knows you are available. Parents always need to separate the behaviour from the teen: **yes, dislike the behaviour but never withdraw your love**. It may seem impossible to believe, but she still craves your acceptance and approval and, most importantly, your unconditional love.

4. Sexuality

Talking about sex can be embarrassing for many parents. It is not enough any more to tell your daughter about the facts of life when she is ten or eleven and then never mention sex again and simply hope for the best. This needs to be an ongoing and two-way conversation. (Sorry!) The more natural and open parents are when discussing sex and relationships, the more relaxed teenage daughters will be.

If your teenager leaves the room every time you try to discuss sex, wait until you have a captive audience – when the two of you are in the car on a long drive and she cannot escape! Make your wishes and values clear and encourage your child to make the right decisions. Help her to understand that having sex does not prove that she is popular and beautiful. Work actively to ensure that she values herself and her future.

We are not saying that teenagers who have a strong sense of themselves and a healthy self-image will be immune to sexual urges, but they do appear to handle them in more mature ways. Strengthening self-image leads to more grounded teens who are more likely to stay involved with family, friends, extracurricular activities and schoolwork.

If you are unsure where to begin, why not talk about how a teenager in a TV programme or film is going through puberty and handling sexual issues. Let your child know how important you think values are. A strong value system can act as a moral compass. It will give your daughter a point of reference. Explain clearly that you hope that she will always maintain her self-respect and respect for others.

The earlier you talk to your teen about sex, the better. Even if you are uncomfortable, think about what you are going to say first because it is important to appear confident, even if you don't feel it. If possible, begin the conversation in a casual manner. Talk about an article you are reading in a magazine or a story you have heard about. If teenagers have open conversations and discussions at home before sex becomes a real issue in their lives then they are better prepared to cope with their emotions and feelings later on.

Teach your child about the emotional consequences of sex. She wants to know that she can confide in you about her feelings. Tell her about your own personal experiences with a first girlfriend or boyfriend; let her know that you understand how exciting these new feelings are and that you are there to listen to her. Much of the information she has gleaned about sex may be incomplete or inaccurate. Lay a solid foundation of trust. Tell her that she can confide in you at all times.

Educate your child about the physical consequences of sex. Teenagers can be more susceptible than adults to some sexually transmitted infections like chlamydia which can lead to sterility. Talk to your daughter about safeguarding her health and valuing her body. Ask her to ask you questions and give her honest and accurate answers. If she feels that she cannot talk to you, give her the option of talking to a family doctor, a relative or another trusted adult. Tell her that you appreciate that having a new partner is exciting, but that she has to find the balance so that family and schoolwork don't suffer. Explain that you are not trying to ruin her life but do put limits in place regarding how often she can go out and restrict computer and phone time. You are doing this because you care.

If your child confides in you that she is homosexual, she may have been working up the courage to tell you for a long time. Your daughter is doing so because you really matter to her and she cares that you know who she really is. It's really important that your child has confided in you and that you are there to support her.

Research groups and organisations in your area. You want to be there for your child, but you may not know where to begin. So arm yourself with information as soon as you can. Listen to your daughter. You love her, she needs to know that. Teach her to have self-respect in whatever relationship she may be in.

Teenage pregnancy

When a teenager finds out that they are pregnant it can be an overwhelming experience for all involved. Although it is certainly not what most teens or their parents envisage, it happens. It can be terrifying and some keep it a secret because they are afraid of how their parents will react. Teenagers need to know that they are not on their own and that they have their parents' support through the challenges that lie ahead. Talk with your doctor. You may wish that your daughter had made different choices. However, by supporting her, listening to her fears and ensuring that she gets good prenatal care, you will find that you can both get through this. You may even become closer.

You never know how strong you are until being strong is your only choice.

Bob Marley

5. Bullying

Bullying can damage your daughter's ability to see herself in a positive light. Female bullies tend to prefer psychological intimidation and isolation, which can have a profound effect on your daughter's psyche. Listening to her when she is being bullied is very important. Never dismiss her words or feelings. Believe in her and support her. Saying things like 'ignore it' or 'get over it' won't help anyone, least of all her. From the earliest possible opportunity take every step to help and protect her from the bully.

We know how distressing this subject is for parents. The teenage years are a time of intense change occurring at many levels – they are particularly a time of great emotional change. If you notice behaviour that is uncharacteristic and believe that your daughter is being bullied, you may wish to seek additional support. Talk to your child as soon as possible and if you find that she is unable or unwilling to discuss what is happening, it may be helpful to link in with her school. Together you can get through this, with the right support and a willingness to keep the channels of communication open.

What can parents do if their child is being bullied?

This book's main focus is to teach teenagers important life skills. Young people can often learn these skills at home with positive and strong parents who love and appreciate them exactly how they are.

- ✹ Let your teen know that it is perfectly acceptable to say 'No', especially if they find themselves faced with a situation which makes them feel uncomfortable.

- ✹ Show fairness at home when dealing with disagreements or conflict. Always listen to both sides and treat all family members the same way. Also, parents, when you argue with each other, try to resolve problems in a calm and respectful way.

- ✹ Make sure that your child knows that sometimes it is better to completely ignore an unpleasant situation and walk away. This applies to very mild forms of bullying and it can be effective. Over time, if the bullies feel that they are not getting anywhere, they may lose interest in your child and move on.

- ✹ Always be a supportive shoulder to cry on. Be there for your teenager and let her know that you want to help her to resolve this problem.

- ✹ Don't be afraid to ask your child how exactly she wants you to help her. She might, for example, agree that it is time for you to call the school. Or she might just want you to pick her up after sports or school so that she can avoid a potentially threatening situation.

- ✹ Always build on your teen's confidence by acknowledging her strengths and achievements.

- ✹ Teach your child to be assertive at home and always encourage her to speak her mind freely and openly. Treat what she has to say seriously.

What do I do if my child is the bully?

It can be difficult to acknowledge our own children's mistakes. Finding out that your child is a bully can be earth-shattering. Your initial reaction may be to defend your child in a misguided attempt to protect them, but it is important to recognise the gravity of the situation. Denying their behaviour and burying your head in the sand will only exacerbate the problem. Call the school as soon as you can – your involvement is vital in stopping the cycle. Let your child know that you are fully aware of what is going on and that their behaviour is unacceptable and will not be tolerated.

Assure your daughter that you will support her. Listen carefully to what she has to say. Explain that bullying of any sort causes pain to others and help her to understand the seriousness of what she is doing. Do your best to uncover who or what may be influencing her behaviour and see if you can understand the reasons behind it. Teach her compassionate ways to work through conflict and understand differences. Explain that there are more positive ways of managing stress and **venting darker emotions** like anger, frustration and insecurity.

Our advice would be to lead by example – talk to her about positive ways that work for you when dealing with frustration when conflicts arise in your life. Ask her to reflect upon why she did what she did, how she herself was feeling at the time and how she thinks it made her victim feel. Counselling may be beneficial for your daughter to help her through this difficult and confusing period.

Cyberbullying

This is an issue which still baffles most parents because it may be an area which they are unfamiliar with. Your child is probably more technologically savvy than you are and way ahead of you when it comes to the complex world of social media. Regardless of this, adolescents need to be taught that bullying is never acceptable and that it can cause long-term problems for those involved.

✳ Discuss this issue with your daughter in an open and non-judgemental manner. Ask her if she or her friends have ever been cyberbullied.

✳ Reassure her that you will not take away her time online. Lots of teens are afraid to tell their parents about cyberbullying for this very reason.

✳ Most bullies do not like themselves and try to feel better by making others feel bad. Explain to your daughter that the bully has the problem, not her. Help her to focus on her strengths and take back control from the people who are doing this. Together you can come through this and emerge stronger and more self-assured than before.

6. Body image

Much to your annoyance or amusement (depending on the mood you are in), hours spent experimenting with hair, clothes, make-up and grooming can become a regular routine for your daughter. As she approaches the teen years, it is natural for her to become fixated on her appearance. As adults, we have developed a more complex self-image which incorporates many things such as our talents, qualities, values and interests. However, for a young person, the reflection they see in the mirror every day is a big part of how they view themselves.

Your daughter may find that she is not always satisfied with her appearance. Media messages have influenced us to believe that you need to look a certain way to be happy. It can feel like a balancing act, helping her to feel confident while also encouraging her not to become consumed with worrying about the superficial. Yes, encourage your daughter to take pride in her appearance but also show her that she has other incredible qualities that are even more important in the greater scheme of things.

Be a good role model. Try to be healthy and positive as much as you can. Never bemoan the fact that you have put on a few pounds. Instead, tell her that being skinny and being healthy are two different things entirely. If you focus only on negatives, the chances are that your teen will learn to see only her own flaws rather than her attributes. Compliment your daughter every day – not only about her looks, but also about all her other important qualities. If she is an incredible guitarist, a graceful ballerina, runs like Usain Bolt or makes the best banoffee pie this side of New York, tell her! That way, she will begin to realise that she is much more than her body.

7. Social media

Wouldn't it be amazing if we could teach teenage girls that everything they need lies within them? That they really don't need somebody in cyberspace to validate their existence and sense of self-worth, because at the end of the day, if they 'like' themselves that's all that matters!

Social media profiles often present a version of the individual which is a far cry from reality. Teens need to be told that what is being presented to them is not always the truth. Although young people can outsmart and outmanoeuvre many adults when it comes to the latest gadgets, apps and websites, parents still have real-life experience to help them differentiate between the advantages and disadvantages of social media. It's up to us, the adults, to help teenagers to use the Internet wisely. We need to remember that teens do as we do. Are you, as a parent, constantly on your smartphone, tablet or computer? What about your social media habits? Be honest, are you setting a good example?

Using the Internet safely

I know that, in some ways, it is easier to turn a blind eye to teens' social media habits. But, long term, this is not an option. It is up to adults to smash through the negative messaging that girls are receiving all the time. It is possible for them to emerge out of adolescence and into adult life with their confidence and self-esteem intact. They need strong, positive role models to gently guide them through these years. Encourage your daughter to be herself, to question what is being presented to her and to never be afraid to speak her mind.

✷ Show your teenager how to use the Internet in moderation. Tell her how to protect herself. Know both her password and user name. Make sure that your teen tells you if she has been intimidated online or talked to in a sexual manner. If you suspect that your teen is a victim of cyberbullying, take steps to deal with this traumatic experience in a supportive and helpful manner (for more on this see the chapter on Bullying).

✷ Students are always being told in school that nothing is private on the net. Remind her of this as often as you can and try to make sure that your daughter's online friends are real friends. Teens need to be aware that once something is posted online it is there for good. Explain that going viral is never a good idea. Also, sexting (sending sexual messages or photos) needs to be discussed. Posting inappropriate material could also have serious implications down the line. Teens often appear to be confident, savvy and worldly wise but while they are under eighteen years of age they are still children. Underneath it all, they are still innocent and extremely vulnerable and they need their parents as much as ever.

✳ Instil in your child the importance of face-to-face, real friendships. Tell her that it is good to talk. Don't be afraid to limit your teen's use of the Internet. Put real guidelines in place. Perhaps you may need to establish a cut-off point each evening. Many students tell us that they are up half the night texting friends when they should be resting. Explain that they can go online for a designated period of time each day.

✳ Ask your daughter not to believe everything she reads or sees on people's profiles.

✳ Help your child see that although social media is an important part of her life it is not actually **real life**. Many of our students have told us that they feel anxious and irritable when they don't have their phones nearby. They hate the thought of missing out on what's happening online because **a lot of the girls feel that real life is what happens online**.

✳ If you have a teenager at home maybe it is time to educate yourself about the world of social media. After all, if you know nothing about this vitally important aspect of her life, how can you hope to protect her from it?

✳ Lastly, and probably most importantly, keep talking to your teen about her online habits. Be interested and not judgemental about her activities at all times.

8. Depression, self-harm and suicide

Depression does not discriminate: it can affect everyone. Teenage depression has nothing whatsoever to do with bad moods or rebellious behaviour – all teenagers have occasional bad patches, but depression is different. It can cause overwhelming feelings of sadness and despair. Inform yourself about teen depression so that you know what to do if you spot the warning signs.

In a non-judgemental way, talk with your daughter about your concerns regarding her worrying behaviour. Make an appointment to visit her GP. Your doctor might refer your daughter to a psychologist who specialises in treating adolescents. Therapies such as Cognitive Behavioural Therapy (CBT) are also very effective. With kindness, patience and perseverance, you can get through this!

Self-harm

Discovering that your daughter is self-harming is deeply shocking for a parent. You may ask, 'Why would my daughter do such a terrible thing?'

Your daughter's life may feel chaotic and like it is spiralling out of control. By injuring herself she may feel she is asserting self-control in her life. It is generally not a suicide attempt but a way of channelling frustration. Those who self-harm tend to view it as a way of coping with life, not as a way of trying to end it. However, repeated self-harm can be an indication of an underlying emotional issue.

Initially, you may well panic and be filled with fear. Your first priority is to deal with immediate medical concerns, and then, when your daughter is willing to talk, listen and try to acknowledge her pain and the severity of her distress. Address what is making her feel this way. Your daughter needs to know that she can trust you and confide in you about these issues. Try not to judge her; instead ask her what she needs from you to help her to get better. If you do need to seek professional help, make sure that you get the name of an experienced and reputable therapist. She needs to know that you love her unconditionally and that you accept where she is at right now. Never make her feel like she is over-reacting. She has to believe that she is not alone and that she has your support. Be honest with her, and tell her that together you will get the help you need to work through this.

Research the behaviour. Be patient and give her time. It can be very hard to resist the urge to self-harm as it can become addictive. It may take time to replace the self-harm with a healthier coping strategy. In order to make a full recovery, develop skills for dealing with the situation and the emotions that lead to self-harm. For example, decide together who your daughter is going to contact if she has an urge to harm herself.

Encourage her to express all of her emotions and her most destructive and disturbing thoughts through positive channels such as journaling, music, art or dance. Of course you will need to keep an eye on her but it is important not to suffocate her. You can encourage her to care for herself by exercising, eating healthy food and getting enough sleep but, the truth is, you can't fix her: only she can do that. With the right help and support she can come through this. Help her every step of the way and, together, you can both move forward. Your daughter will get better. This will not last forever.

Suicide

This is something no family ever wants to go through. Teen suicide is a relatively rare event; however, when suicide does happen, it is heart-breaking for all involved. All families deal with the aftermath of an attempted suicide differently. Some parents bury their emotions, while others can suffocate their child by never letting them out of their sight.

After a child attempts suicide, families desperately need support and direction. Shame, guilt, denial, bewilderment and anger can prevent them from seeking out the help they so desperately need. It can be confusing trying to figure out the best course of action. Try not to focus only on the suicide attempt, but also on what else was going on in her life that may have caused the attempt.

Be there for your daughter. Let her talk whenever she needs to and actively listen. Do not be judgemental, as this will discourage her from opening up to you. Your daughter is probably feeling incredibly lost and unsure about her future; she needs your support and unconditional love now more than ever before.

Professional help is essential. Working with a psychiatrist, she can learn to develop the ability to exert control over her suicidal feelings. Therapy can be difficult and painful, but it takes time to work, so encourage your daughter to keep going.

It is natural to worry that she may make another suicide attempt. However, you cannot let this worry consume you or prevent you from getting the professional help that your whole family needs.

Maybe together you could make a survivor box where your daughter could put in anything that she associates with comfort, such as letters, poetry, pictures, movies, objects or music. It is important that the things she decides to put in remind her of how wonderful, valued and loved she is. So, whenever negative thoughts begin to take over, she could go to her survivor box and focus on the moment in hand and not let fears of the future overwhelm her.

No words can describe the pain of losing someone to suicide. No matter what happened, it is imperative that you understand that the suicide is not your fault. Your loved one chose to end her pain in the way she saw best at that moment in time. There are so many questions, but no real answers. Blame will not bring your daughter back. You may never understand the logic or reasoning behind what she did. Acknowledge all of your emotions; get the help you need to move through them. Do not go through this alone: seek professional help.

Eating disorders

It can be very difficult to talk to your daughter about her eating disorder, especially if she is still in denial. However, it is essential that you persevere, as communication is essential in her recovery. Prepare in advance what you plan to say and, regardless of her reaction, it is important that you remain calm. Be considerate of her feelings. Do not be judgemental. It can be difficult for your daughter to express her feelings behind her eating disorder. At first she may not open up to you, but be patient and listen carefully to what she is trying to say. Ask her what you can do to help her. Be honest with your feelings and encourage your daughter to do the same. In order to understand what you are dealing with, you should find out as much as possible about eating disorders. Assure your daughter that, no matter what, you will always be there for her. You need to contact your GP and find the best professional help possible. You can be the responsible parent your child needs you to be. Your daughter needs you now more than ever.

9. Academic pressure and study skills

When did average ability stop being good enough? The desire to have a genius in the family can be a real problem for teens. As parents, we want our children to be successful and we want to be encouraging and supportive. Parents can be made to feel that they are not doing enough if they don't pressurise their children to succeed in a cut-throat world of careers and education. As a result, they become so focused on pushing their children to achieve that they miss the golden opportunity to connect with them properly. Instead of listening, we are directing; instead of joking and having fun, we are constantly bemoaning middle-of-the-road grades. Maybe it's time to accept that there are very few geniuses in the world. If your daughter is working hard and doing her best, this is good enough.

Academic pressure is one of the most common pressures that teens deal with on a daily basis. As high-achieving students push themselves further and further, one starts to question: how much is too much? Of course we need to foster a sense of achievement in our students, but parents must find a balance between encouraging them to succeed and putting their mental health under strain. The objective is to help our children to thrive and not just survive.

> **(S):** I vividly remember a bright, diligent student crying one day as she confided in me that she fully understood why her parents wanted her to do well in school, 'but sometimes I feel under so much pressure, as I know they are disappointed in me even when I have tried my hardest'.

Here are some ways to encourage your daughter while avoiding putting her under unnecessary pressure.

✳ Parents say they push their children because they want them to achieve good grades in order to secure admission to university and then get a stable job afterwards. However, academic excellence isn't the only measure of success. Remind your daughter that having a high IQ does not mean that she will automatically be a more employable individual. A strong work ethic combined with skills such as flexibility and the ability to work in a team have as much effectiveness as being able to speak Mandarin.

✳ Of course you should support and encourage your daughter – but don't pressurise her with unrealistic expectations. Your child is a success when she has done her best. Life is about dealing with both failure and achievement. So, what lessons are we teaching when we accept nothing but straight A's? Instead, praise her for things that she can change – like her level of effort or the strategies she can use.

✲ Are you the type of parent who lives their life through their children, chasing your own unfulfilled dreams and unrequited ambitions? Teenagers should be free to follow their own North Star, their own dreams and ambitions, not those of their parents. Love and accept your daughter for **who she is and what she is passionate about**.

✲ Try to find the balance between caring and caring too much. The real measure of success is a happy, successful, secure and well-balanced child, not one who obtains off-the-Richter-scale grades but is secretly unhappy and stressed beyond belief.

The best way to make children good is to make them happy.
Oscar Wilde

10. Anxiety and panic attacks

At different times, everyone experiences anxiety in their life. This is a natural emotion, but sometimes it can become an all-consuming and unhealthy response. It can leave teens feeling completely immobile. When emotions such as fear, panic, worry or avoidance strike, teenagers can be left feeling that they are destined to live this nightmare forever.

Anxiety is a manageable and treatable condition and teens learn to overcome it with the right help and support. By helping your daughter to understand societal pressures and equipping her with the skills which she needs to persist in times of stress, you are giving her what she needs to live a meaningful and balanced life.

Parents can help teens to rise above negative thoughts and feelings. Children learn positive thinking patterns by observation. One of the most effective ways of teaching teens is to model a calm and positive attitude yourself.

A panic attack is an episode of severe anxiety with emotional and physical symptoms like chest pains, nausea, dizziness, shortness of breath and sweating. It is a terrifying experience and can make some teens feel like they are having a heart attack. Certain symptoms may trigger the panic attack but they also occur without any noticeable cause. A fearful anticipation of when an attack may strike can set in. This is completely understandable but in extreme cases can result in teenagers avoiding situations that they fear may trigger an attack. Reassure your daughter that by practising the various techniques discussed in the teen section on anxiety, she can handle it.

Along with getting enough sleep, eating healthily and exercising regularly, teenagers need to learn skills to soothe and calm themselves when stress and anxiety strike. Developing coping skills now will carry her throughout her life. Learning to be mindful and live in the present moment can make teens feel more in control of their lives. Cognitive Behavioural Therapy approaches can help your daughter to examine and manage her anxiety.

Thinking negatively about life can be detrimental to your daughter's mental health and well-being. Confidence, along with positive thinking, can guide her down a very successful life path. Be patient and try to pinpoint and understand the specific anxiety triggers for your daughter. Address underlying issues. If problems persist, seek medical help.

11. Critical illness/grief and loss

We are all complicated individuals who feel, think, act and react to life in our own particular and unique ways. When a loved one is seriously ill, teenagers can feel overwhelmed by loss and bewilderment and may not know where to turn.

How do I tell my teen that a family member or loved one has a serious illness?

We know that there is no right or wrong way to start a difficult conversation like this. However, young people value honesty and may want to talk openly about what is happening, while others could become withdrawn and appear aloof. Everyone responds differently to news of this kind. Your daughter is simply coming to terms with it in her own way. She may need time to process her feelings. Be patient with her. She needs to know how this will affect her life. Our advice? Tell her as soon as the diagnosis is definite.

Anticipatory grief is a very real emotion and occurs when a loved one is diagnosed with a serious illness. Difficult emotions such as denial, sorrow, anxiety and anger may rise to the surface and it is very possible that your daughter will struggle to cope with these feelings. Encourage her to talk. Open-ended questions like 'what do you feel about …?' can help. You do not need to know all the answers. Explain that you will update her as and when things occur and remind her that you are on this journey together. It might be helpful to inform your daughter's school so that they can support her also.

If you both feel up to it, why not create a memory box? This entails decorating a special box containing photos, letters, songs, DVDs or memorabilia that are important and will help to keep a loved one's memory alive long after they have passed. We understand that even thinking about this may be overwhelming, but the actual process can be deeply satisfying as it affords your daughter the opportunity to connect with the memories of her loved one and all the wonderful times they shared together.

How do I help a teenager cope with the death of a loved one?

We have found over the years that teens need a good listener, not a lecturer, so they can express their emotions. Don't try to 'fix' your daughter. You need to let her go through the grief and pain in her own way and at her own pace. When you listen with your heart, you can respond compassionately, and this way you can help her to work through her feelings. Phrases like 'it is time to move on' or 'you must be strong' leave no room for discussion or exploration. It is better to use open statements that invite your teenager to talk honestly about her feelings, like 'This must be very hard for you' or 'I'm so sorry – do you want to talk to me about how you are feeling or how I can help?'

An important part of the healing process is remembering the person who died in a way that is meaningful. Your daughter may need a lot of affection at this time or she may wish to be left alone. Do your best to validate her feelings. Appropriate boundaries and discipline are still important because young people need to feel safe and secure during this chaotic and confusing time.

Although they have experienced a traumatic emotional blow, kindness helps teenagers to realise that they are not alone, that they still have support, friendship and love. Small gestures can express great compassion. Be available for them. Look up support groups in your area; they can encourage teenagers to share their loss in a non-judgemental environment and can help them to discover the strength to carry on.

12. Separation and divorce

Although no one plans it, divorce sometimes is the only option for a couple. This is an extremely difficult time for all involved, but especially teenagers as they struggle to come to terms with what is happening. Your daughter may not be able to express what she is going through with you – it could be the case that she simply cannot articulate her distress because she might be afraid of hurting you even more. If this is the case, try to make sure that she can talk openly with someone she can trust.

As a parent you need to look after yourself also if you are to care for your family properly. By all means find emotional support but whatever you do, avoid burdening your daughter by making her your confidante. Do not use her to communicate or say hurtful things to your ex.

Keep communication as open as you can. In order to reduce feelings of confusion and anxiety, give adequate explanations about the separation and involve your daughter in decisions that affect her. She needs to understand that she is not the cause of the separation – that what has happened has occurred between you, her parents. Listen to what she has to say and let her know that you will both always love her and care for her. Do not ask her to make decisions that involve choosing between parents. Ensure her emotional hurt is eased with care and support, not with material gifts or lack of discipline in the home.

It can take a while for your daughter to work through her feelings and adjust to the separation. Be patient with her. A range of strong and upsetting emotions may surface such as shock, embarrassment, fear and anger. Accept this and tell her that this is part of the process and is very normal. However if you are concerned about your daughter's safety and welfare, seek professional help. Inform the school and other significant adults in her life so they can support her.

And finally...

We believe that the two most important things that parents can give their children are roots and wings. All parents want the best for their children – of that we are certain. However, the teenage years can be a steep learning curve for even the bravest among us. As parents, it is easier to give your child roots – you work long and tirelessly to provide your daughter with a safe and comfortable roof over her head. Wings are harder to give, because even though she may look and act like a strong and independent woman of the world – in your eyes, at least, she will always be your baby girl.

It can be downright difficult at times coping with an adolescent as she embarks boldly, and at times infuriatingly, on her journey of self-discovery. It may seem beyond your ability to let her go, but remember, if you insist on holding a beautiful butterfly in the palm of your hand, you will ultimately hinder its flight. Know that, although she is testing the limits and pushing through boundaries, eventually she will emerge out the other side of adolescence as a responsible young woman who takes your breath away and who you will be proud to say is your daughter.

We believe that if you do your best to create a positive family environment which enables her to negotiate adolescence with as much ease and as little distress as possible then you are already doing a great job. Deep down you know that, no matter how crazy your daughter makes you, she is worth every minute and if you had to go through the pain, chaos and confusion again, you would do so in a heartbeat.

Useful Numbers

Aisling
Provides advice and support to parents who have children affected by alcohol and drug abuse.
Phone: 046 907 4300
www.aislinggroupinternational.ie

Alateen
This organisation provides support for young people aged between twelve and twenty years of age who are dealing with a problem drinker.
Phone: 01 873 2699
www.al-anon-Ireland.org

Aware
This organisation provides support for people suffering from or affected by depression. If you feel depressed or are worried about a friend or family member, Aware offers a listening service whereby you can discuss your concerns in a safe and non-threatening way.
Phone: 1890 303 302
www.aware.ie

Barnardos and Child Bereavement Counselling Service
Looking after young people in Ireland.
Phone: 01 473 2110
www.barnardos.ie

BeLonG To
Provides support for gay, lesbian, bisexual and transgender young people from fourteen to twenty-three years of age.
Phone: 01 670 6223
www.belongto.org

Bodywhys – The Eating Disorders Association of Ireland

An organisation which provides support for people dealing with eating disorders.

Phone: 01 283 4963

www.bodywhys.ie

CARI – Children at Risk in Ireland

This organisation provides services including therapy for children, teenagers and their families who have been affected by sexual abuse.

Phone: 1890 924 567

www.cari.ie

Childline

This is a 24-hour service offering support and a listening ear for young people up to the age of eighteen.

Phone: 1800 66 66 66

www.childline.ie

Console

If you have lost a friend or family member to suicide, Console offers bereavement counselling and support.

Phone: 1800 201 890

www.console.ie

Grow

Dealing with mental health issues across the country.

Phone: 1890 474 474

www.grow.ie

Life

This helpline provides support and a non-judgemental ear to women dealing with the distress of an unplanned pregnancy.

Phone: 1850 281 281

www.life.ie

Pieta House

Pieta House is a non-profit organisation that provides specialised treatment for people in suicidal distress or engaging in self-harm. They run the annual 'Darkness into Light' event.
Phone: 01 623 5606
www.pieta.ie

Rape Crisis Network

Provides support for victims of sexual assault or harassment, rape or child sexual abuse.
Phone: 1890 77 88 88
www.rcni.ie

STI clinics

www.ifpa.ie/sti/clinics

Acknowledgements

The inspiration for this book comes from all the wonderful and inspiring teenagers we have had the honour of teaching during our thirty years of teaching. We couldn't have written *Shine* without you. You have taught us so much about life and made us laugh out loud every day. To you we say a big and heartfelt – **thank you.**

A very special mention has to go to all the current students in UCT, especially our sixth and transition year classes of 2015. Again and again we quizzed you about how teenage girls view the world and every time you told us exactly what you thought and how you felt. The future of this Fair Isle is in very capable hands.

To our families who have been part of this journey. Thank you for all your encouragement and patience and for believing in us from day one.

To all our friends and colleagues in the Ursuline for your enthusiasm, friendship and goodwill. We would like to give our principal, Mary Butler, a special mention because not only did she proofread *Shine* for us but she was as excited about the book as we were.

A heartfelt thank you to all at Hachette Books Ireland for taking a chance on two complete unknowns and giving us the opportunity to follow our North Star and chase our dreams.

To our fantastic editor Ciara Doorley for her brilliant insights and amazing enthusiasm for *Shine*. and of course to Joanna, for her incredible patience and dedication.

To Siobhán Doorley who set the wheels of *Shine* in motion. We are forever grateful.

To Martine Madden, for your advice and support from the beginning. We really appreciate your friendship, honesty and expertise. Thank you.

We definitely cannot forget Conall Mallen who opened our eyes to the possibilities and allowed us to believe that anything was possible.

To our dear friend Siobhan McQuillan for your beautiful mandala drawings which brighten our book. You always instinctively knew what we wanted. What a cover!

To Shane for all your help and Doireann for your words of wisdom while critiquing a very messy first draft. In many ways, your analysis gave us the confidence and determination to keep going.

To Dermot Bannon for all your help and support in the early days. Thanks a million.

To our dear friends everywhere: you know who you are! Thanks for always being around through all the good times (as well as the bad). You have given us something that we will always treasure: fantastic memories.

Lastly, to Liam, Amy, Ava and Grace, our reasons to shine and to the two wise men, Damian and Ray – this book would not have happened without all of you. Thanks from the bottom of our hearts; this one's for you.